NEUTRON GUN RELOADED
A Gerry Reith Reader

Neutron Gun Reloaded: A Gerry Reith Reader

Nine-Banded Books
PO Box 1862
Charleston, WV 25327

ISBN 978-0-9907335-9-1

Foreword ©2020 Denis McBee

Introduction ©2020 Chip Smith

Special thanks to Bob Black, Anita Dalton, and Ivan Stang.

Cover design by Kevin I. Slaughter

CONTENTS

Foreword by Denis McBee ~ vii
Publisher's Introduction ~ xi

Part One (Quixote)

The Roots of Modern Terror~33 • To Rust Unburnished~36 • Foreign Policy~40 • Fraud, Cheat, Lie, Thrill~49 • Twilight to Authority~53 • Kings of Orient, Dresden, D.C.~57 • John's Adventure~63 • Cost/Benefit Equations~69 • Rodeo Week in Sheridan~77 • Singularity~79 • A Brief Overview of Our Activities to Date~80 • The Devil's Day Off~87 • Revisionist History for Children~93 • More Revisionism~98 • Winning Hearts & Minds~102 • Melpomene's Little Sister Georgene~107 • Digressions~112 • Drifting in One Spot—1~115 • Drifting in One Spot—2~119 • Family Notes~124 • Formulas~129 • Being Against Motherhood Does Not Go Over in Peoria~132 • Once I Thought I Knew~135 • That Then I Scorn to Change My State~138 • K. Goes to the Lecture~140 • Case Studies~143 • Number 8, Number 8~150 • Sensations~154 • Conflicting Virtues~157 • Kidnapped!~161 • Issues in Suspension~163 • Variations on a Theme~165 • Closing Redux~170 • An Objective Lesson~176 • The Pleasure Palace: A Visit~179 • Third Worldview:~185 • DILIGENT Historians…~189

Part Two (Cervantes)

Post-Mortem~195 • Art Rant~202 • Science Fiction: Overrated~205 • Quixote: How to Use~210 • Manifesto Notes, 1~215 • On *Factsheet Five*~219 • On *Processed World*~223 • Bad Company: *Oath of Fealty*~226 • Communication…~232 • An Introduction to SubGenius Theology~234 • The Problem in the Church Today~242 • Prelude, True Anecdote and an Observation~247 • Untitled~250 • Doctor, Doctor, Fix Me Up~255 • Untitled~256 • Punk, Meet Suburbanite~257 • Nighttime for the Postman~261 • Letter from the Graveyard Shift~265 • The Usual~268

Gerry Reith Bibliography compiled by Bob Black ~ 276

Neutron Gun Reloaded

FOREWORD BY DENIS MCBEE

The Long Slow Burn of Metaphor: Power of Story and the Resurrection of Gerry Reith

Gerry Reith first sent us a manuscript in 1981, his response to an article in our second edition of *Beatniks From Space*. Publishing an underground literary magazine back then was loads of fun and we were clever rascals on the local party scene. A thousand miles away, however, a complete stranger was reading carefully. Gerry's polemic was an early indication that someone over the horizon was paying attention.

By the spring of 1982 we had received a substantial batch of Gerry's writing and I suggested that he consider a book project. We had just published Reith's "Cost/Benefit Equations" in Gregory Altreuter's *The Death Collection*, a chapbook that pondered our chances of survival in a world of indifference. Gerry's first response was to propose a sequel to the Altreuter project. His concept quickly evolved into what became *Neutron Gun*.

Gerry Reith's *Neutron Gun* was a catalytic call to action. Thoroughly commanding the stage, Reith challenged his audience to not remain stuck in the mud of their comfort zones, to face up and disengage from ennui. His tools were not the chiseled precision of fancy words nor the elegant diagramming of a perfect sentence but the long slow burn of metaphor—and the power of story.

Neutron Gun was first published in 1985, a second printing appeared in 1987. For a host of reasons beyond the scope of this discussion, the Neither/Nor editions of Neutron Gun were flawed presentations. I made a long series of bonehead decisions, and with reckless exhuburance, ineptly executed a ridiculous business plan. A few years later the Neither/Nor Press crumbled in disarray. Gerry Reith's book, as with all of our publications, fell out of print.

The powerful metaphor and call to action of Gerry Reith's Neutron Gun survives intact. The energy that flows between writer and publisher and reader, expressed over a vast expanse of geography and decades of time, moves forward like the treads of a tank or bulldozer grinding through the mental landscape. That flow of energy gave an unsettling urge to an aggressive new publisher who steps in to move the project forward. This Nine-Banded Books edition gives the writing of Gerry Reith new standing in a new century. This is resurrection.

Denis McBee
August 11, 2020

...last stop before hell or Sheridan if you're gonna stay alive for a while.

"IN XANADU, TO BE AN INDIVIDUAL ONE MUST BE A CLONE."

—future proverb

WHO IS GERRY REITH?

NO ONE KNOWS. None of Us, anyway. But They know. And so MINITRUE's tireless belletrist, parablist and liberterrorist faces the faceless minions of illuminist intrigue. Yes, the taxman cometh, and we must stuff his putrid maw.

WHO IS GERRY REITH? This much we know: he is

— Anarchorexic;
— A dualist duellist;
— Furious at Fuehrerists;
— A curt Anglo Saxon;
— Tired of Trilateral tyranny;
— Manichean depressive;
— The mailman's reluctant best friend.

SURE, we have our little differences; we wonder if Austrian economics leads to Austrian politics; we watch with concern as he William-Burroughs from within the Liberaltarian Party. But Reith reads "between the lies"; he composed Beethoven's 9th Amendment; he hasn't aroused Their wrath for nothing!

LET'S PREVENT A ROCKY MOUNTAIN HORRORSHOW. Let's show Gerry Reith that there is a free lunch, perhaps even a Naked Lunch! To assure that he gets his licks in (and gets Prolixin), to make sure that Reith hasn't sterilized his last Mason jar, send money today. "The sleep of reason begets monsters," so wake up! To each according to his needs!

BEWARE MASONIC MIND CONTROL TECHNIQUES!

NOVUS ORDURE SECLORUM

a public service announcement from
THE LAST INTERNATIONAL

Publisher's Introduction

Requiem for an Invisible Warrior

Picture Sheridan Wyoming. Your first impression.

Start with Big Horn peaks set against vast horizons. A crystal-blue firmament, or if you prefer, the star-dusted canopy of night. Nested within the lazy sprawl of cattle ranches and postcard vistas, the town itself offers such rudiments of civilization—a grocery outlet, some barbecue restaurants, dim-lit taverns, shops showcasing western memorabilia—that suffice to satisfy the needs of a small population as well as the slow stream of tourists, many (not all) of whom will look forward to Rodeo Week and attendant festivities. Local charm, local color. You know.

Daylight now. Nod hello to passersby as you stroll down Main Street. They are a friendly lot and their eyes won't be fixed on the screens of mobile devices because the year, I neglected to mention, is 1984. This is important; go ahead and revise Your Own Personal Sheridan accordingly. The automobiles should be backdated and decorated at your discretion with legible signifiers. Maybe some Reagan/Bush bumper stickers? That Starbucks will have to go. Otherwise, not much will have changed.

Continuing on your mind's eye ramble, you come to a community bulletin board outside the small, nondescript Post Office. Look at those flyers. All in all, it's a familiar collage. Tourist that you are, you first notice the ones that advertise local farm and ranch services. It's mildly exotic, yes? But there are others that might be found in any American city or town. Lost pets. Babysitting services. Guitar lessons. Et cetera. Do you find this comforting?

Look closer.

Displayed among the random patchwork of community ephemera, there are ... oddities. Being a punk sophisticate from the future, you may recognize the hand of a subversive poster artist, Xerox as medium.

"TRUTH IS LIES" shouts one banner that lassos your attention.

Another asks: "WHO IS GERRY REITH?"

High weirdness resides in the fine print. But let's not get ahead of ourselves.

How, you might rather wonder, in the heart of Cold War Reagan country, might the *locals* have received such provocative broadsides, such cryptic expressions of obliquely dissident satire that, for a time, blotted their dogpatch town-center pastiche? Were they mystified? Amused? Bemused? Were they—some of them—given to a moment's reflection?

More likely, they took it in stride. *Some kid's idea of a joke.*

Still, you wonder. Perhaps your borrowed understanding of the Markov Chain comes to mind. A state change in the system. A disruption. You fix on the idea of a white current rippling through a multi-hued sensory order, a neural rift that bleeds between minds and forward through time, disturbing equilibria.

It is best, for now, not to dwell in such idle speculation. For present purposes, there is more to see.

Mosey your way into the lobby of the Post Office proper and imagine what voices might have carried on a particular day—let's say April 23rd, a Monday, and my fourteenth birthday—as you sidle up to the counter where one postal clerk can be overheard chatting up another.

You don't catch all of it, but certain words ring clear. Something about a backlog of *weird mail* for that *lanky dude* who until recently arrived *like clockwork*. And perhaps another clerk calls in answer:

You mean Gerry, right?

Something is amiss.

The postal clerks will soon receive the news and the plastic tub of unclaimed mail—*weird mail*—will be stamped and returned as dictated by protocol. "Recipient deceased: Return to Sender." Inquiries may follow from official channels on high, but the ground-level postal employees will receive little information about such intrigues. Rumors will circulate, soon to be forgotten.

As to the curious flyers outside, they will be removed in time, or just as likely tacked over with more quotidian fare. "Rodeo Lessons: Best Rates Guaranteed!!!"

This is how I choose to imagine it. Yet we still need to close the scene—if only for the benefit of those who have only recently arrived.

Shall we make it a movie, then? Go like this.

From the postal lobby, start with a slow reverse tracking shot back out into the sunlit exterior. Flash-dissolve to a crane shot and rocket up in a vertiginous sweep to settle into a long bird's eye panoramic view of the town center. Slower now, let's float over the quaint metro-western townscape until we fix on some certain near-enough dwelling below. It might be a room in the Veteran's Center. Or a bungalow.

Now coast then arc into a sharply accelerated descent, perhaps with an acrobatic tilt and glide to and through a keyhole for maximal CGI-enhanced cinematic effect.

You can devise the trappings of the interior scene thus disclosed (books and strewn paper will surely be part of it—and a mid-game chessboard, please), but the centerpiece, best revealed through a creeping Steadicam crawl like what you vaguely remember from the opening sequence in *Pink Floyd: The Wall*, will be … *The Body.*

It is *slumped over a typewriter* (not a word processor) at a *writing desk* (not a table).

Somewhere next to the body—or clutched in hand—will be *The Gun.* Go with a revolver, I insist.

Such is the core of our marginal legend. Certain canonical details must be observed.

The rest will be determined by your tolerance for gore. What remains crucial—per the canon—is that we zoom in on the *sheet of paper* that, at some point prior to blowing his brains out, the writer cum body had fed into the typewriter. The words—the writer's *final words*—on this page cannot be made out. They are obscured under a *stain of blood*. Or viscera, brains, gloop. As you like it.

End of sequence.

Maybe it was a word processor.

Maybe it wasn't a revolver.

Maybe the words were legible. Was there even a note? It is my understanding there was a note.

By all reliable accounts, it was indeed a suicide.

On April 7 1984, in the small city of Sheridan Wyoming, Gerard Bennet Reith died at his writing desk of a self-inflicted gunshot to the head. He was 25.

The catalyst for Reith's suicide may have been a ludicrous (but apparently real) FBI inquiry into his voluminous mail correspondence with radical elements. Or it may have been, as I am more inclined to believe, an acute passage of unrequited love. One story has it that Reith compiled a ledger to weigh the pros and cons of existence, ending the exercise with the fateful flip of a coin.

While the details of Reith's act of self-deliverance remain hazy and subject to apocryphal embellishment, the work he produced during his apogee as a writer for a raft of underground publications left an indelible impression in the minds of those who discovered it. Consorting at the bleeding edges of what has since been described as the "marginals milieu" of the pre-Internet era, he traded arts and letters with a motley coterie of avant garde outsiders—neo-dadaists, libertarians, anarchists, egoists, situationists, primitivists, nihilists, Xerox pamphleteers, conspiratologists, SubGenius pranksters, and sundry anti-authoritarian shit-stirrers of polymorphous pedigree—whose only real alliance distilled to a spirit of freewheeling creative rebellion.

Athwart and among these misfits who inhabited and cultivated the mail-order demimonde that preceded Anonymous and the chans and cryptocurrencies and 3D-printed guns and Less Wrong logomachy and neoreactionary jabberwocky and incel manifestos and such other manifestations of digital mindfood and mindfuck that would later complicate the Spectacle, Gerry Reith produced essays and criticism, poetry and prosody, broadsides and collages, but most notably short stories and metafictions. And his work—especially the stories—invariably stood out. Reith's best writing was marked by mordant wit and controlled experimentation, but the cumulative gravamen of his variegated literary and epistolary endeavors was to interrogate and celebrate the prospect of freedom in a universe governed by venal agendas and brute entropy.

Though Reith's literary output spanned a range of literary and visual forms, he is perhaps best remembered—to the extent that he is remembered at all—for his works of short and sharply honed allegorical fiction, many of which found their way into the pages of the first Neither/Nor Press edition of *Neutron Gun*, a posthumously published collection that presented Reith's often violent parables alongside the work of a few kindred spirits.

I first read *Neutron Gun* when I was a teenager. Like so many formative book-centered experiences of my aimless youth, the slim volume came to my attention through the back pages of the Loompanics Unlimited book catalog. If I tell you now that I recall being mildly disappointed by the total package, I will in the next breath emphasize that I would return to those pages—and later to Reith's other writings, which have been dutifully archived by his friend Bob Black on the Inspiracy website*—time and time again in the years and decades that followed.

True, there was a roughness at the edges, a zine-like presentation that fell short of the post-punk aesthetic that I sensed as aspiration. And yes, the central propulsive force of Reith's signature prose seemed awkwardly juxtaposed against the voices of other contributors. But if the barker's pitch ("*more than just a book, this is a concussion device…*") initially struck me as being a mite

---

* http://www.inspiracy.com/minitrue/bio.html

overwrought for what was, on first and later impression, a collection of stories, I had to admit that it was no ordinary writers' workshop assemblage.

"To Rust Unburnished" was a sort of Russian doll meditation on societal entanglement and mortality salience, where you get shot dead by a clown and the show goes on. "Foreign Policy" presented a parodic account of an intimate struggle session, a *pas de trois* of dialectical upmanship that reveals the grimly hierarchical precepts that govern political—and *sexual*—discourse. In "Fraud, Cheat, Lie, Thrill," the staid environs of a used bookshop become the epicenter of anarchic revelry, culminating in the ambivalent promise of creative destruction. "Twilight to Authority" was a cryptically intoned cautionary tale of dormant idylls brought to a reckoning, and "Kings of Orient, Dresden, DC" could be read as a kind of pre-*Matrix* red-pill allegory, casting the plight of the individual against the rapacious sprawl of the managerial state. Perhaps with a sly wink toward William S. Burroughs (as well as, explicitly, John Zerzan), "John's Adventure" limned a memorably violent (and gorily comic) spectacle to expose and lampoon the primitive impulse festering beneath and within the veneer of civilized rat-race ritual. And "Cost/Benefit Equations" was a hardboiled tale of insurrectionary bloodwork, seen and unseen.

No, these were not MFA scraps. Reith's stories had a pulse. They added up to something. He wrote with preternatural urgency and control, fusing metaphor with action. He dealt in lean, high-impact, rapid-fire shock-and-awe. Eschewing prolix and pretense, the interconnected parables Reith signed for *Neutron Gun* were resonant with wild energy yet anchored by beat narration and breezy erudition. His stories—or *fictions*—converged upon a comic-nightmare vision of social distress and upheaval and inexorable collapse. In mood if not specificity, he tapped into the quickening pulse of "peak everything" derangement that social critic James Kunstler would later describe as "The Long Emergency," a condition now realized in the riotous mediagenic reel of post-pandemic global fear and loathing. Yet more relevant to our present predicament, Reith anticipated the catastrophic groove—if not the Baudrillardian verbiage—that now ramifies in the memetic churn of accelerationist discourse. Decades before Nick Land would wax obscure about the "hyperstitional dynamics" attending crisis-mode late capitalism, Reith's parables captured the essence of what was coming, festering, waiting. He saw it like an elegant chess sequence, plotting the moves.

In shades prescient and perilous, Gerry Reith inscribed a world on fire ("What fire? There isn't any goddam fire," says the drunk; "Fires aren't dangerous" says the Captain), and with ironic implications that would flare yet brighter in the long afterburn. If he has claim to a posthumous legacy, it is oracular; with his ear to the

Wyoming ground, he divined apocalyptic rumblings that have only grown louder.

It would be easy enough to stop at this. As a safely impressionistic retrospective drive-by exegesis, we could do little worse than to acknowledge that the kid was ahead of his time and leave the heap for contemporary perusal. Yet there is a counterbalance to Reith's infernal tableau, both literary and implicitly dialectical, that 21st-century readers would be remiss to ignore. Within the texts of *Neutron Gun*, the sleight is suggested in a countermanding spirit of gleefully insurrectionary exhortation—in tales of factional strife and internecine assassination plots where human relations encode a trenchant revision of Sartre's hell. If the prospect of meaningful liberation stands a chance against a faceless instrumentality, the ties that bind—i.e. our fraught connections with "other people"—are what remain. "We're all painfully self-conscious Hamlets," he wrote, "yearning after the kind of closeness only achieved in Conspiracy, love, or war." A rope is not always a noose, comrade.

Reith's prick-kicking gambit comes into sharper relief as we stray further from the reservation, to take in the longer view that comes through an appraisal of his formative range as a writer and thinker. While the core of a vaguely remembered gallery showing in the pages of the only short book that heretofore bore his posthumous byline—the *concussion device*, as it was sold—retains a certain *sub terra* mystique as our central attraction, the young man had far more to say, often in a different key. What's on the other side of the *Gun*? One purpose of the present volume is to bring the buried wreckage into view.

I was tempted, as you would be, to cordon off the densely imbricated storyscape that comprised Reith's driving presence in *Neutron Gun*, to preserve and present the late scribe's singular curatorial arrangement as a matter of precious archival posterity. As postmodern conventions permit, we might even retro-conceptualize it as a *novel*, right? I suppose that option remains for future archeologists, but I feared it would be a hairsbreadth shy of treacly nostalgia.

Worse, it would fail as tribute. From this temporal distance, I believe a finer degree of postmortem appreciation is achieved by considering Reith's broader body of writing—his more enigmatic allegories and tales, his Carveresque lowlife vignettes, even some essays and poetry—within and against the grain of the *Neutron Gun* exhibition. This *disjecta membra*, as fate has determined, now serves to illuminate the once-thriving potential of a literary career that was, I'm sorry, just getting started.

The broader terrain is marked by prose-poetic flourishes and spiritual residue, by kitchen sink realism and bold experimentation, by mirth and myth and mayhem and mystery. And there is a commanding insight that stretches across forms; whether he is deconstructing the façade of Western masculinity or weaving an entrancing fable about a vanishing secret order of monks who guard the world from suffering and sorrow, Reith's footing is sure and his human portraiture, even in caricature, is seldom off the mark.

I am especially fond of "Satan's Day Off" (a sort of subversive Faustian shaggy dog story depicting the Dark Prince as a beleaguered worldly rambler in search of a kindness), but the germinal promise of Reith's protean literary peregrinations can be located not only in counter-mythical tales and cyphers but in autobiographically situated sketches that drew upon his workaday experience, respectively as a motel clerk and as a slumming denizen of a run-down veterans' outpatient rooming house. Such vignettes cast the narrator as a kind of in-field observer of embattled humanity, where Reith's pneumatically attenuated anti-authoritarianism slyly merges with the Sartrean ploy to break a lance against "the bureaucratization of all social relations."

A banged-up morality propels the disparate experiments and threads. Alone at his writing desk, Reith fought an invisible war; he saw the tanks approaching even as he cavorted among those who claimed not to know about the tanks. And like the errant Don Quixote, he tilted. "In the end," he wrote, "we are all Quixote; what we forget too often is that we are also Cervantes." Smuggled within that preciously descried duality, I believe, is a shimmering paradox. As our best dreams are sullied in the grime of shared humanity, corruption brings us closer. Another chess sequence, perhaps. And yet, like the imprisoned Cervantes, we must answer to the gaoler. For now.

Look, I fretted interminably over this fucking book, and I'm not entirely sure why. After I got the greenlight from Reith's former editor Denis McBee, I thought it would be a cinch to knock out a "kitchen sink" compendium. The guiding impulse was simple enough and the same as always: I wanted the book to *exist*. In corporeal form. I wanted it to be a *thing*—another thing—to be discovered and held and examined and pored over and studied as books are, or were. I figured it would be a straightforward task, a simple matter of cut & paste underground press bricolage—with the *Neutron Gun* matter front-loaded (as if in a jeweler's display case) and the remainder appending (as if in a cabinet of curios). Done and done, yeah?

Apparently not. I perseverated. I procrastinated. And I *worried*.

I worried over how it should be presented. I worried over what should be included. I worried over what should be excluded. I worried over notes, fonts, dimensions, design. I worried over the reaction of lingering elders. I worried over everything.

Looming large was the matter of *biographical scaffolding*. Not a lot of information is available concerning the life and times of a self-styled Connecticut Yankee cum Wyomingite anarchist bohemian who lived and died in the American West years before I dropped acid, and recondite accounts were already discoverable online. Should I, as a matter of due diligence, reach out to Reith's surviving friends, family, and erstwhile correspondents to pry for such reminiscences and commentaries that could serve as framing? Such an approach might have been advisable, or perhaps obligatory from a certain editorial perspective. But, no. Those people are now old (as am I). Would they be in a position to reliably channel the spirit that stirred among their number memory-sifted decades ago? Would this even add value? More likely, you'd get nostalgic encomia, anemically tinted survivor stories and who cares. Gerry Reith was born in Connecticut. When he was a teenager, he spent some time in a psychiatric facility. Then he moved to Wyoming where he got some college. He played in a rock & roll band. He wrote. He blew his brains out.

Which brings us back to the matter of *Reith's suicide*, another worry. Here we find a salient hook and lure, something just as conspicuous if it were ignored. Trouble is, it always translates as convenient literary romance, or again worse, as a kind of morbid rebrand. I suppose I'm already guilty of foregrounding Reith's untidy end, however ironically, at the start of this regrettably fatuous introduction (for which I apologize). But is there evidence of suicidal ideation in the work itself? Always a fair question. Plot it out as you're inclined. *I have to get out or I'll die*, said the nerd punk perched on a plank. Highlight the clues, the references; there are enough to make hay—or a dissertation for all I care. The problem will remain that from a safe and cozy reading nook far from a bloody mess that had to be cleaned up by somebody long years ago as tears flowed, we will absolutely fail to apprehend the underlying anguish. Ultimately, the living are better advised—and happily liberated—to look elsewhere. If you want to trace a thread of gloom all the way down, read Jean Amery, or David Foster Wallace's footnotes. Stick with the mythos in its plastic contours and you'll find the heartbeat. Or draw up your own ledger.

Then there was the matter of *correspondence*. In a sense, everything that Reith wrote was grounded to an overarching epistolary project, being an extension of his commanding presence in the nascent marginals and mail art scene that we now must squint to remember. But if we separate honed craftwork from the prolific chain of letters and missives that appeared in the pages of sundry zines and Amateur Press Association collations and local newspapers, I think the distinction is fairly delineable. Enough for roadwork, anyway. To be sure, there is much of interest in these ephemeral texts, many of which may be consulted on the web. Reith's letters provide a window into the forming trajectories underlying his truncated development as a writer. His game-theoretical (and curiously psychoanalytic) cerebrations over chess strategy; his engagement with

Russian novelists; his jaundiced take on science fiction; his digressions on Ayn Rand, Thomas Pynchon, John Fante. Et cetera. There is insight to be gleaned—but such that would be of more interest to a presently nonexistent biographer. Divorced from contemporaneous context, it's so much distant thunder.

I also worried over *aesthetics*. Was Gerry Reith a writer who dabbled in visual confrontation? Or vice versa? I insist the answer is clear, yet the "Minitrue" Xeroxiana that he produced remains a relevant and instantly recognizable component of his creative output. The provocations that I imagine to have been postered outside that Sheridan Post Office can be informatively positioned alongside currents of counter-media displays that trace back to Situationism, to Discordianism, to Stewart Home's Neoist brand, and trace forward to the unwoke corners of a percolating online alt-whatever memeplex. And that Sheridan kid, we may admit without shade, often did it better. For present purposes, however, it remains a peripheral attraction. You know my answer.

Finally, there was the matter of *politics*—or "The Political" as gravely rendered by Carl Schmitt. Frame this with the full-stop concession that Reith's work was and is inescapably political—as in: governed by questions of stake and the prospect of transformative violence; as in: concerned with the *polis*. His abiding mission, expressed across his literary and aesthetic endeavors, was to expose and decode and strategically oppose the agents and chimerical instruments of authority. I hesitate to characterize his stance as a sort of antinomian anarchism, but I don't know what shoe fits closer. In an informative 1986 essay for *Boston Review*[*] Bob Black offered a more textured account of Reith's evolving political dalliances and proclivities, but it still feels like life-lust anarchy to me. It is perhaps worth noting—as Black does—that he was active in the Wyoming Libertarian Party (as nominal VP and editor of the house newsletter), and that he cut his chops in anti-nuke activism. But I wouldn't read too much into that. Reith's affiliations and communications were expansive and eccentric, as befitted a seeker. The gestalt aligns to unfettered *individuation* rather than rule-bound individualism, or hazy communalist froth. Stirner more than Bakunin, then—with a dash of Kropotkin resonant in passages on the prospect of abolishing hierarchy, lest we become "just another coven of cops." Choose your own adventure. I'm pretty sure he didn't like gun control. Or cops.

In the end I decided to roughly divide certain differences while resisting my initial temptation to mine for autistic completism. Gerry Reith was first and foremost a *writer* and this, consequently, is a primarily a *literary* collection. With some close-call exceptions that I may

---

[*] "Mailing Their Way to Anarchy." *Boston Review*, August 1986. http://bostonreview.net/archives/BR11.4/black.html

come to regret, the stories and other writings now on offer are presented not as time-stamped remnants of some bygone subcultural efflorescence, but as a thematically cohesive showcase of a largely forgotten body of work that reverberates *now*.

However I've botched it, at least it's a fucking book.

So we kick things off with a none-too-subtle paleo-accelerationist parable, providing an apt segue to the core *Neutron Gun* texts that immediately follow in minor though considered rearrangement. For those who want to experience the effect that frankly belongs to a different time and mood, some residual impact is thus, I hope, preserved. Appending this cluster-bomb with no hard break are Reith's other lapidary "fictions"— pitched in perhaps subtler tones, but centrifugally anchored to themes that decipher either as politics or discontent or frolic, often in some volatile combination.

The next section consists of nonfiction, and this is where you will find a spare selection of Reith's crafted essays, including "Post-Mortem" in which he articulated his wild ambitions for *Neutron Gun*, and "Quixote: How to Use," an insightful essay that informs the structure of this volume. Though I cut swaths of material that seemed dated or precious, some dusty reviews and couple of Reith's SubGenius screeds are presented mainly as evidence of his critical nous and a dexterous command of deepfake satire. We close with some poetry and a couple of letters that screamed forward through time.

If you want the Full Monty, you know where to look.

Reith's original publisher, Denis McBee, who politely stopped asking about this project long ago, was kind enough to provide the foreword that precedes this long-winded opening pitch. I want to thank him for everything. I also want to thank Ivan Stang of the Church of the SubGenius for dispatching sacred church texts, even if these didn't make the cut. Finally, from a safe distance, I want to acknowledge the diligent work done by the anarchist contrarian wordsmith Bob Black, who has for years maintained an online archive of Reith's extant writings.

Had that fabled coin flip gone the other way, Gerry Reith might have gone on to create greater things. But what he left behind is what we have. We don't get to call it juvenilia. And that's alright, because it sings.

Chip Smith
August 31, 2020

PART ONE
(Quixote)

Metafictions
Allegories
Parables
Sketches
Prosody

. . .

The Roots of Modern Terror

You are among the many passengers of a large bus careening wildly down a twisted mountain road. The bus is being driven by a drunk who is half blind. He and those near the front are also suffering from some sort of intoxication from gaseous emissions. They are also drinking. It is night; not even the moon is out to provide lighting. The main lights of the bus are broken from near-brushes with the steadily deteriorating old guardrails that are the only thing between the bus and a 2,500-foot plunge off a sheer face cliff.

The bus is traveling at a truly high rate of speed, etc. Evidently the brakes are out. *Only* the screams of watchful passengers have kept the sleeping driver from crashing. Within the last few minutes more than four times the bus has had a near miss, headed straight forward into a sharp turn.

It is raining and the roads are slick.

You originally got into the bus to obtain protection from the elements. This was long ago; so long that you don't remember. Way back when, some wise guy started the bus, and began driving. The drivers have been changed several times, but no matter what, they all speed up; they frequently promise to slow down some; and they all drink heavily from seemingly bottomless flasks stored near the front.

Most of the passengers sit, mute, staring off into space, rolling out of their seats and not getting back into them. They seem paralyzed. Those that still seem conscious are divided. Most of them believe the bus is headed somewhere. So do the drivers. But others know that there never was any particular destination in mind. A while back you and some others found a map, inside something called a "history book," and on the map was a picture of a road. The map has clear markings that say "Dead End." In fact, it is a deader end than most; the map indicates that the road ends in an abrupt, unmarked precipice.

Some of the passengers want to get out but the windows and doors are welded shut. When they go up front to talk with the driver or his supporters near the front, who are also drunk, they are forcibly pushed back. Shouts have one result: the driver speeds up, and slumps over the wheel more frequently. Some of the passengers think that everyone should be quiet and enjoy the ride. Others are positively certain the driver should speed up. Still more don't even think the bus is moving.

Once in a while a passenger goes berserk, doing great physical harm to those around him in attempt to go and seize the wheel.

According to the map, you are not far from the end of the road. Most of the people who are told this become immediately agitated and call for new drivers. They then attempt to go and take the wheel, which causes the present driver to swerve and screech around in an even more chaotic way. You just want to stop the bus and get out, but you cannot. To no one else has it occurred to stop the bus. And it seems those in favor of speeding up are gaining the upper hand; they are driven by the idea that if they get there faster everything will be okay.

To Rust Unburnished

A reader sat reading—it was Mr. Harris with an old mystery. He sat in one of a million conceivable rooms of a city, bored witless. One of the three 60-watt bulbs in his overhead lamp had burned out earlier in the week; every time he turned it on for reading he got the sensation that he was going blind. "I'll have to buy a new one soon," he thought; but if he'd had a wife of ten years, she would by now have learned that he wouldn't buy any until they all burned out late one night.

It was the same with his television—the tube had burned out, what, a year or so ago, and he never got around to having it fixed. The radio worked though. "After all," Harris told Jones at work, "I don't do anything when the TV is on, I just sit there."

"Ah, ya just sit there anyway," Jones replied. "My kids watch it all the time." He scratched his cheek, letting his eyelids droop. "I don't see how they get their homework done."

"It's the schools. How do you know they even get homework these days." Harris smiled. "Who cares, eh?"

The mystery revolved around a book theft, some rare

old Elizabethan folios. A literary scholar was called in to consult with the detective. They sat for lunch. "Do you know," the scholar asked the detective, "why the literary figures of the period are often shown with a human skull on their desks?"

"No, why, I never thought about it," Harris read.

"Well, because many of them did keep skulls around." The scholar smiled. "They were called a memento mori, a death reminder. The point being that we all end up there sooner or later, so why not live in the present, get cracking?"

The detective was alert. "Seems like that wouldn't work," he said, "for people who don't have any vision." He sipped his coffee, the meal over. "I mean, these guys knew their strength, when they looked at eighty years it was no time at all. Nowadays…" He spun his hand at the wrist, trying to get the general picture. "Well, with nothing but trivial concerns, all that time is just a cross to bear. You know."

"Eighty," said the scholar. "But in those days you were an old man if you made forty-five." He paused. "You're right, though. It's easy to drift with external currents. And they definitely were not holding stopwatches against themselves." He rose to leave, the detective was getting up. "By the way," he asked suddenly, "about the case, can you find a clue in the world?"

"The possibilities are endless. All we have is an outline right now." The detective brightened up and chuckled.

"You know why those guys died early?" he said. "I hear Marlowe used to drink wine the way we drink beer."

Harris looked up at the clock. "A beer would be nice right now," he thought, putting down the book.

Just then a knock came at the door. Harris walked over and opened it, finding a man in a clown suit with a gun, who aimed and fired. In Connecticut, at the Ruger Arms warehouse, a shipping clerk was talking to his girlfriend on the phone.

"The clinic said I was pregnant, Joey."

"Well, what do you want me to do about it?"

"I don't know," the doctor told his nurse. "But I think we'll need the inventory sheets first so we can make out the claims for the insurance people to go over when they get here."

"It's a terrible time we're living in," she replied, shaking her head. "No one pays attention to what our creator wants any more." She glanced down at a copy of *Babelwatch* open on her desk. "Drug Scandal Rocks High Circles," it told her. The article's author was masturbating in Mobile, Alabama, the latest issue of *Spermbank* magazine laying spreadeagled before him on the bed.

The object of his attention, the Account of the Month, Miss May, was at that moment in class at the local business college in America, learning sales analysis, an eternal golden braid in her hair.

"The time preference factor serves to explain interest

rates in micro-economies," the teacher told them, closing the book on his desk and standing up. "The vendor of credit has to avoid the 'Scylla' of idle resources and the 'Charybdis' of liquidity problems, all the while seeking the highest rate of return." He gave a start when the bell rang, and turned toward the wall.

"We have at least one person here who understands about making use of her god-given capital," he said, turning back and winking. "There's a world of opportunity out there." He wagged a finger at them. "Potential waiting to be realized."

Foreign Policy

1

One dark and glistening night, while I calculated percentages and busied myself in other ways, I was visited by two friends, Sergei Glup and Debbie Development.

Sergei liked Debbie very much, and wanted to get in her shorts. I suspect he rather wished I wasn't present because then it would have been easier to tell her so. Although god knows why, since I was hardly in the competition, and we were all on relatively intimate terms.

They engaged in conversation, ignoring me, but preventing me from doing my work.

"I'm an authority," Sergei would announce.

"Oh, I don't know about that," Debbie might reply, coyly.

At other times the exchange went like this:

"I'm an authority."

"Yes, I see. Maybe you are after all!"

Sergei seemed to think that if he could finally establish his authority he might have a good chance of getting Debbie into the boudoir with him. This was hardly likely, but they spent much time detailing the requirements to be met by all those who would be allowed into bed. Sergei made sure that all his categorical qualifications included Debbie, or someone like her; Debbie offered that her standards were pretty high.

At times I made the mistake of commenting.

"'Love' as a word often confuses the issue," I said at one point, adding: "What we're talking about, in the abstract, are the delicate negotiations that occur…the two sides allow each other to save face for as long as they both want the bargaining to go on. They beat around the bush trying to con each other with vague terms, thinking it's diplomatic. Say one wants the other to be at his beck and call while the other doesn't like the idea… these types of conditions are established, perhaps, by gossiping about others…"

I was interrupted by a wave of the hand from Sergei, who translated for Debbie, telling her, "I'm the authority around here."

It carried on like this. Once in a while I popped in and got minor slaps on the wrist to remind me to keep my mouth shut unless I had something to say that would augment Sergei's standing.

2

After a while I grew sleepy, although I was keeping an eagle eye out, practicing. It was entertaining to consider the combinations, and it gave me a thrill when my silent predictions were fulfilled. But my tiredness led me to make the same mistake over again: I kept commenting, and they began to focus on me.

In a politically related discussion of motive, I couldn't let them continue with the hogwash they were spouting; if I had it would have meant complete capitulation to a doctrine I don't hold, and I would at some future point have been called on it. "Oh come on," I said, "People basically do what they want to, within certain limits."

That's when Sergei really cut loose. It was more of an error than I at first supposed, because it should have been obvious that Sergei wasn't doing what he wanted to do by any stretch of the imagination. He got angry, probably imagining that I imputed to him some lack of desire to pork the babe in our midst.

"What do you mean, certain limits!" he roared. "Anything can be within your supposed certain limits!" If there wasn't a rug on the floor he might have spit.

"You conveniently ignore the operative clause and seize on the qualifying one," I snapped back, irritated that he would have the effrontery to escalate but even more irritated at myself for failing to have seen what was coming. "I'm talking about not going out for a Reese's Peanut Butter Cup when you've just fallen into an earthquake divide! It's by definition, discovered in retrospect, that's all! They do what they want to because if they didn't do it they didn't want to!"

It got worse. Sergei pulled out all the stops after seeing my acrimony. He interrupted me, not allowing the last words to be heard, and said my proposition was stupid. After he had finished (he said, "That's stupid, that's stupid!" twice), he talked about contradictory motives and hierarchies of desire, and I threw in a contemptuous statement to the effect that, if an action be taken, one value has by default taken precedence and can be viewed for these purposes as the prime motive in the case.

Then Sergei drew an example, which I demolished; he said that someone who writes a bad check for a hat they want has contradictory motives and isn't really doing what they want to do. I nearly laughed out loud, recalling Freud and wondering if this example didn't have some bearing on his relationship with Debbie. It appeared to me to be quite simple, that what he meant by confused motive was the event-description of lies. One lies to oneself so as to lie more effectively to the other person. Sergei had designs he couldn't reveal.

But what I said was that, in the first place, error in judgment is not mutually exclusive with volition as the *sine qua non* of action; and that, in the second place, people who aren't fucking autistic generally know the results of their fucking actions and in fact desire those fucking results.

But Sergei wouldn't brook the idea that some people enjoy being unhappy, even when I backed it up with the proof that exhibiting symptoms of unhappiness is a common tactic for eliciting specific responses from others.

He began getting incoherent and continued insulting me, asked what I was talking about (to which I threw in, "Commenting on the bind," which was ignored), and somehow devolved into asking me why I was disagreeing with him.

"I was defending a statement!"

"What statement, what statement!" he yelled, evidently having an adrenaline rush and thinking that if he could get me tongue-tied over some particular he'd have won a victory valuable enough to offset the cost to his dignity of having stooped to such a tactic. I suppose it had become a case of getting me to shut up at any cost.

I realized too late what I had done, and that now the process had become a contest to the end since Sergei was out to re-establish authority and had nothing to lose. Not wanting to lose too much myself I decided to cut it off, get it over with by resigning, and I waved my hand in dismissal and shut up. There was no way I was going to get in a fistfight, and this was probably the next escalation.

After a few minutes during which Debbie respectfully listened to Sergei as he cleared up such questions as why people die with smiles on their faces and whether this was proof of an afterlife, Sergei turned back to cauterize my lips for good.

"You were resisting," he said, somewhat calmer. "You got irrational, and you wouldn't listen to me because when people get to the, ah, root of the irrationality of their position, they get emotional. They get more excited the closer you get to their point of vulnerability."

Besides projecting, (it was beautiful, clinically perfect), he was giving me more reason to suspect that he actually was familiar with police method from spy interrogation training, and he was showing an interesting ability to forget what don't come in handy, like the Marin County Relationships jargon he'd been spewing earlier; if he truly thought he had me in a corner, according to his Beauty of Personhood Becoming bullshit, he would have backed off. But this stuff only comes into play when bamboozling a potential piece of ass. Then again, some of the other schools of new age thought apparently hold that the only way you can be friends, really friends, with somebody, is to dominate them at every opportunity, destroy their defenses, leave them no privacy, secrets, or pride.

I was somewhat more irritated at this point than I had been throughout the meat of the contest, mainly with myself because I regretted ever having challenged his authority. I wasn't a contender for the girl, yet I had put our friendship to an unnecessary test. I suppose that the demand for equal footing on an intellectual basis was misinterpreted as a demand for equal footing in the quest for lonely ova, probably because Sergei was using his intellectual prowess as a selling point.

Anyway, worse was to come, because I had made a dual error and exposed myself to discovered check. Debbie turned on me with this cutting motherly line, seeing she could fend off the invites tactfully by scoring points on me. This way she could bask in the cheap warmth of being desired by keeping negotiations open... which was her only interest, since anything beyond negotiation was going too far for her taste.

"What would you say if I told you that I love you as you are," she began, making me wince, and evidently dismissing from memory her sage nods at my explication that 'love' is a worthless bargaining chip, seeing as how it remains undefined until the trump is played, and even then is defined by the person who first anted up. "...But..." (and here the buzzwords came thick & fast) "...you cannot ever be my political leader. You're too young, your ideas are too radical, but I'd like to keep a dialogue open with you even though I don't plan on ever agreeing with you on any particular, especially the important ones and you will in fact be wasting your time to talk to me, but I know you'll never let your frustration show because then I'll be able to hit you over the head for having hurt my feelings." In all, the raving took about five minutes, and five minutes of acute discomfort are a small price to pay to stave off a month-long campaign. Sergei stared at me to gauge my facial response to the onslaught, so I did my best catatonia, making with the blank stares, which is known in the trade as clamming up or diminished affect.

In the end I shrugged, since the thrust was clear before she had finished and I'd had time to figure out which act would neutrally signify recognition that it was over. Her pitch constituted an insult the likes of which I have seldom received, and they both thought they were loving friends…It was almost terrifying. I sat still for a while. Any material counter-attack would have given them an excuse to resume the fusillade.

Moving around while they babbled, collecting coffee cups and straightening up papers, served to get them standing and moving towards departure. They both knew it was getting late and I wasn't done with my work. They haggled over the literal content of religion (which keeps some people busy for centuries), mostly to the effect that Debbie hoped to get the newly-ordained authority to endorse her delusions about god and happiness when you're dead.

As it turned out, Sergei tired of this before Debbie did, perhaps realizing that he'd been taken for a ride. He bowed out, and Debbie stayed on to repeat her line about not having the slightest respect for my politics, but at the same time wanting to keep an interesting whipping boy or clown to call on for occasional entertainment, and by the way, proofs of god, reincarnation, and similar patronizing shit.

I did my best to keep writing at my desk and patently

ignore her, but she really must have had a blood lust. She went and made a new pot of coffee and brought a cup over to sit and drink it while reciting some disordered litany. I stopped working and listening long enough to formulate the necessary shrapnel grenades.

"Look," I said with a fierce glare and a commanding tone that was unusual between us but functional now that I was bent on ridding myself of this insect as quickly as possible, "All you are trying to do is find some smart people who will tell you that what you read in crank paperbacks is true. You continue to refuse to look at the uses of your beliefs despite the clear necessity of doing so when evaluating them overall. I find it obnoxious that you try to pester me into sanctioning this bullshit consolatory prattle. Go away and drown in your doubts if you want to, I'm not an authority to be called on to allay your fears, quit harassing me."

"H'm…" she said, at a loss for words. Not long after, she left.

I recalled the time when I had given Sergei's brother, Rinzai, a briefing on the content of Jay Haley's masterwork, *Strategies of Psychotherapy*. "H'm…" he said, at a loss. Maybe if Jo'Shu had said it.

"Yeah," I carried on, ignoring the *H'm*. "When I read it I thought I'd never be able to carry on a normal relationship with anyone ever again." But who wants to? Hierarchies are the norm here in human-land. In hierarchies, as they say, you either lick boot or kick face.

Fraud, Cheat, Lie, Thrill

Sissy was just closing up shop when the telephone rang, it was her old friend Ariadne, who asked her not to lock the door. "Stay open another half hour," she said. "I'm only in town for a while and I'd love to see you."

The only sale Sissy had made that day was a copy of *The Book of the Book* by Idries Shah, so staying open had more than one virtue to recommend it. The rent was due soon, and when it was paid there wouldn't be much left over in the checking account unless something like the sole proprietor's salary was left out of the budget. She smiled to herself grimly. "Well," she thought, "I can always do a little street-walking if this doesn't work out." Closing up meant counting the till and making out a bank deposit slip, too often, like tonight, unnecessary.

A secondhand bookstore wasn't always a paying proposition. But parents die and even small windfalls are good excuses to quit selling yourself and enter the dream world. Sissy had always loved browsing through those stores in out-of-the-way corners, looking for a rare and forgotten jewel, maybe some out-of-print work by Proudhon or Stirner, in fine leather binding, available for a song. Now, running one, she fell in love with every oddball who came in asking after an obscure title that they shared as a secret, a wall that the mystery and romance buyers would never cross. Those people weren't buying books, they were buying warm glasses of milk to help them fall asleep at night. Imagine a diamond merchant doing the bulk of his trade in costume jewelry!

At a few minutes after five a flood of people came through the door, speaking French. One came to the counter and asked about where they could find more bookstores once they had finished here.

Sissy shrugged. "I'm all there is," she said.

They busied themselves inspecting titles and pulling books off the shelves with sighs and exclamations. Sissy perked up, since they were likely to buy. She saw one of them drinking openly from a flask and noticed from the corner of her eye as more customers came in. The crowd began to get boisterous, with actual shouts of surprise, "No one has this book!" "Look, look here!" And so on.

Ariadne came in with some beer.

"Drink with me, Sissy, drink!"

Sissy accepted a beer and asked what had brought Ariadne to the city.

"Abortion. By the way, you don't have a copy of *Dubliners* around, do you?"

"Sure, over there on that shelf," Sissy pointed. "What

made you interested in Joyce all of a sudden?"

"Oh, this clown down at the clinic told me to look it up." Ariadne drifted off toward the shelves and Sissy found herself drinking alone. The place was packed.

Sissy opened another beer and accepted a shot from the flask when its owner came to pay up. All she had was a coffee cup and the shot was more like a scotch on the rocks with no rocks. "Drink, drink with us!" the man yelled. "Yours is the best store we've seen in ages!" He raised his arm, swung it out, and shouted over the uproar. "A toast, a toast to the finest of the fine!" Everyone seemed to have a drink in hand. Music was coming from somewhere. "Who is that, Wagner, right?" Sissy asked the man with the scotch.

"Yeah," he answered. "I think it's *Der fliegende Holländer*."

More people came in. Sissy could hardly tell how many because she was busy making change for the ones who wanted boxes and bags full of books. There didn't seem to be any order to it. The Frenchmen were buying anything and everything, it didn't matter, they must have gone crazy for American books. Sissy felt drunk and noticed that the lights were going on in the streets outside. Someone even wanted to buy the painting on the wall behind the counter, a scene of crows in a cornfield by some unknown artist.

Ariadne came back and laid her purse next to the phone on the counter. "Would you take over for a minute?" Sissy asked. "I'm getting tipsy, I can't count anymore."

"Sure, why not?" Ari giggled. "Why don't you eat something, here." She reached into her purse and drew out a pomegranate. Sissy took it and ate a bite. She then passed out, the gabble of voices rushing and roaring in her ears.

When Sissy woke up Ari was asleep on the floor next to her and people had been making change on their own. The shelves were empty, but a pair of lovers lay in one corner, busy with each other. A few stragglers came up to pay. All they had to offer was bullets. Opening the drawer, Sissy found it full of lead. She screamed at the last people, "Get out, take what you want, I'm yours now, you win, get out." A manic leer split her face and she ran out into the street, threw a rock at the glittering neon sign of a store nearby. It blew out in a truncated flash and she stood there.

Twilight to Authority

It isn't clear why but for some reason the Council of a Thousand Minds was called to deliberate over the situation.

And such a minor case at that. Why we all remember when the Council used to sit in semi-permanent session and occasionally publish proceedings. Weighty tomes, multiple-volume sets issued over the years; we saw them in obscure libraries and appreciated the habit we have of surrounding ourselves with excuses for awe… "Here," we might say, "is the assembled wisdom. Here is where the great have dealt with the Questions." And we all knew that while some people were cut out for it, we just couldn't afford to read that stuff. We flattered ourselves that with the sort of effort it takes to quit smoking we could master some portion, but this never proves necessary when popularizers make a living at translation.

The Council hadn't sat, for…well, how long now? Not being newsworthy, it drifted out of focus, and the king had his ministers…There's rarely much of a market for bearded old men from around the world who mutter to themselves and slowly, delicately come to the conclusion that while *Yes* has its benefits on the other hand *No* certainly merits consideration.

Now, inexplicably, the eyes had turned. Perhaps it was the spirit of the hour, and something you did not without realizing it had caught the attention of a major figure who lived in secret exile from what he regarded as distracting bustle. You were living simply, unacquainted with the extent to which you had assimilated vital currents, unaware of subtle implications that charged your every act with an elegance invisible to the monoconscious. Once, during different days, a fashionable notion had currency: that it were possible for certain individuals to embody a world idea or personify some key Cause; —sometimes they were right—but now... it is a new Time. It is the sort of time, perhaps, when the embodiment of a world idea can live in squalor and possess grace without knowing contrast. Maybe when obscurity and fame no longer cancel but complement each other; when, mysteriously, those few that can Know begin rediscovering fine distinctions which the busy and trivial most invariably miss.

However, it may be you didn't suspect that your manner was likely to attract attention. It always seemed that everyone acted more or less the same in certain fundamental respects and that we all made mistakes of about equal importance, and for the most part this is true, except that your mistakes were correct mistakes somehow...they were exact, precise. You were calm in the face of their consequences, wielding an invulnerability.

Then came the arrest, the ordeal. Your trial would be approaching and your innocence may have been spent by others to buy a form of surety, perhaps. The prosecuting attorney began calling at night to offer abuse; the stress of complicity in fraud showed even in the cracks of his face. But the defense was cavalier, distant, unreachable, possessed of a confidence he couldn't communicate.

During this same period you were spotted, and it seems at times as though there is a conspiracy of people trained in arts next to which sub-rosa CIA recruitment looks like dancing when compared with making love. Some group vaguely infiltrates the social matrix, going native; then forgets itself automatic like a virus of indeterminate periodicity. Potential crosses a gap somewhere, triggering a shifting cascade of contingencies, catalyzing metamorphosis into another obscure high definition. The latticework shivers and then re-crystallizes, suddenly aware of the mission intrinsic; from imp interstitial to keystone of arch in one quantum step; among other things, lines of influence reopen as might ancient riverbeds taste new rain...

With the trial coming up and the degradation it would entail, you couldn't imagine what use it would be to you for some peculiar party of conspirators to find you and whisper; but then we all heard that the Council had been called, with astonishing mandates of speed, unanimity. There was a connection.

They gathered and held the Chess tournament which determined who would serve as moderator. Days passed. Hermetic sessions were held while the countryside buzzed with rumor. Data was requested and at one occasion you were summoned to present yourself for questioning which was smooth and polite: the Council won your heart with the charm of old men who know that what they do is of paramount irrelevance. They treated the upcoming trial almost as an afterthought but as weeks passed and the courtroom scene approached, you suffered. Would this Council never be done exploring the exigencies of Catastrophe Theory?

Word came; a messenger was sent. You didn't need a cryptic note and didn't get one, but the content was not meant to be revealed. You told me, but I guessed. (Ah, Melpomene.)

Kings of Orient, Dresden, D.C.

When I woke up the place was on fire. I didn't know where I was. Smoke and flames everywhere.

I ran around screaming, trying to find a way out. The hallway was burning. My hair caught on fire. Somehow I made it to the cellar. I remember falling down some stairs.

An old drunk was lying in the corner.

"Help!" I shouted. "Help! Fire!" Even down here you could smell the smoke, like when the wind blows round your campfire. Crackling sounds from upstairs nearly drowned out my voice.

"Huh? Wha?" the drunk mumbled.

"Look! I'm burned! Fire! We have to get out!" I yelled in his face, started shaking him.

"Let go!" He twisted around. "What fire? There isn't any goddamn fire." Orange light from the far wall lit up his face.

"Just listen! Look around! The ceiling! Gonna fall on us! Which way do we go?"

He stared at me. "Look, sonny," gruff, bleary. "There isn't any fire. You're acting like some kind of radical.

Bug off! Lemme alone." He looked at an empty bottle on the floor, made a face.

Drunk and stupid, I thought. The pain came back, and I grabbed him. "Just tell me how to get out of here!" I shrieked.

His arm swung up and bashed me in the head. "Out! Talk sense if you're going to talk! What do you mean, out?"

He was bigger than me, so I ran.

∞ ∞ ∞

I found another stairway and went up. Couldn't breathe to run any more. Heat made me sweat. Too thirsty.

One of the doors opened. Another guy was standing there. "Hey!" he said. "Where are you going?"

"Don't know! Help! On fire!"

"Calm down!" He was stern. "I know there's a fire. You're not burning now. Just sit down."

I sat. The floor was hot. "How do we get out?" I asked. At least somebody knew what was going on. Something crashed nearby.

"We don't," said the guy. "We wait here for the soldiers. They're busy pouring gasoline. The worst thing we can do is panic. We have to stay put and stay calm."

"But, but..." I was still breathless. "We'll...get... burned..."

"Maybe so, but that's a risk we have to take. There's no

reason to worry."

I heard more beams crashing. Then it hit me. Gasoline? "Why are they spreading gas!" I yelled.

"To put out the fire, you idiot! Why else would they do something like that! They ran out of propane!"

"But we're trapped!" I stood up.

"Shut up!" He was feeling the stress.

"You're getting hysterical! I don't know! Just keep quiet!"

I couldn't stand it. I just started to laugh, and cry. My hands hurt where they got burned. I hit him, then I ran off like crazy.

∞ ∞ ∞

I don't know where I went. The fear got worse. I was alone. A door blew out right after I passed it. The blast burned my back. I was frantic.

Then I got to a hall with an indoor pool. I ran straight for it.

There were soldiers. "Stop!" they called out. I kept going. They grabbed me. The lake was crystal clear, still as stone. I screamed and bit them and tried to get loose.

"No, no! Help! Help! Let go!"

They wouldn't. Everything popped. I gave up. Who cares? I started to cry. They dragged me to an office.

The captain was there. He was on the phone. Papers all over.

"Well," he said after a while. "How are things?" He

didn't look up from the paperwork.

"I hurt all over," I said. "What about the fire?"

"Oh, that. You must have come from one of the primary infiltration quadrants. We're safe here." He chuckled.

"The water. Why aren't they putting out the fire?"

He frowned. "They didn't tell you much, did they? When the soldiers put water on the fire it burns hotter. Besides, we're not supposed to put it out."

I stared at him.

"We have to keep it going, don't you see? That's why we're here. I coordinate the placement of the gunpowder and the hydrogen."

"Did you start the fire?"

"Well, not exactly, no." He paused to light a cigar. "The higher-ups did. There was too much phlogiston."

"Oh."

"The scientists over at the planning center found out about it. Sheer chance. It's all too complex for a man like me." He started chuckling again. "Funny about the planning center. Computer printouts keep catching on fire. They're having a devil of a time staying on top of the phlogiston calculations."

"Why don't they run?"

"Why should they? Fires aren't dangerous. Studies show it. A million times we'll see a fire that never even bothers us. The chances of any one fire ever doing actual harm are so low that it's absurd. Everyone blows it out of proportion." He frowned again.

I was tired of all this. "Can I go in the pool? Just for a while?"

"Oh, no. I couldn't allow that. What good would it do?"

"But I'm burned!"

"But you're just a single person, my boy. So what if you cooled off? You don't even exist outside the context. You might throw the phlogiston calculations way off." This was deep for him.

"Can't I go to the hospital, or something?"

This made him laugh. "I'm sorry. They really didn't tell you anything. We had to burn all the hospitals, during the airlift. All the phlogiston flowing around near the patients. It would have started something without warning. We're burning the whole city. If we didn't, it might catch fire."

"The whole city?"

"Yes, yes!" He was growing impatient with my questions. "Don't you see! If it caught fire without warning it might spread! Don't you realize what a responsibility this is? We have so much trouble."

John's Adventure
(For J.Z.)

John heard a scream and looked up only to see a body rushing toward him. He stepped out of the way just in time and nearly vomited when his face was spattered with blood. The impact was solid—one of the limbs flew off, and the entire skull flattened out like a vase might.

I have to get out of here, he thought. Looking up again, he was amazed to see that another person had jumped, or been pushed. He started to run. Ahead of him, at the next intersection, a man was walking out into the street even though the light was red. Before John could yell "Watch out!" a limousine plowed into the jaywalker, with startling force. Contorted into strange angles, the body flew up into the air and landed on the roof of the limo, bouncing off and finding rest behind the bumper.

The limo had stopped in a squeal of brakes. Now John heard another loud horn as a business van skidded, rocking back and forth, before the loud smack and grinding crunch as it struck the limo. The force of the van caused it to roll over, and another unlucky car served to absorb the momentum.

A fire broke out, and there were shrieks and loud moans. Then a gas tank exploded and the whole intersection was a giant inferno. Cars continued to smash into each other in a parody of chaos. Sirens sounded in the distance, adding that peculiar edge of panicky glee to the scene.

"I'm not going to cross that street," John said to himself. He decided to go into the bank to his right and watch from behind thick windows.

A shot rang out as soon as the door had closed behind him. Then another. A gruff voice yelled across the room. A woman begged for mercy. The robbers, evidently, were angry about the accident in the street because now their getaway route was cut off. They had decided to slay the occupants of the bank in retaliation for their bad luck, and were doing so with alacrity. John left the way he had entered, quickly.

Out on the street again, he walked back to the scene of the high jumps and pushed his way through the crowd. Now there were six bodies in various states of explosion, and one more was on the way. Everyone around John was gasping, delighted and disgusted.

Freeing himself from the spectators, he walked on and managed to make headway for a few blocks. Across the street there was a roar and the sound of tinkling glass. A wave of hot air nearly knocked him off his feet and John started running when he saw that the bomb that exploded had also started a fire on the first floor and threatened to bring the entire building crumbling down. It was an old building, noted for the unusual tilt which a settling foundation had imparted upon it. The structural stress was too much, in fact, and John stopped and stared for a moment as the ancient brick walls gracefully dove into oblivion. The cloud of dust engulfed him as he turned and walked on.

A voice called to him from out of a darkened doorway. A woman was there, yelling for help, being raped by a large black man. The rapist looked dangerous so John moved on, figuring that rape prevention was of no consequence any more.

Pretty soon he got home. Sitting at his kitchen table, he glanced at the newspaper headlines. DISASTER STRIKES IN SMALL MIDWESTERN TOWN, said one. CANNIBALS APPREHENDED, STOCK MARKET CRASHES said another. All of a sudden the door was kicked in.

It was a policeman. "You are under arrest," the policeman said.

"What for?"

"Don't worry about that now, just come along with me."

John contemplated resisting, but it would be futile as the policeman was waving a gun in his face. As he stepped out into the hall, he saw that everyone in the building was being arrested.

"Look here," John said. "What's this all about?"

The policeman read him his rights and slapped a pair

of handcuffs on his wrists.

"You are under arrest for second degree complicity."

"Complicity in what?"

"Ask the judge, big mouth." The cop gave him a slap in the face. "And don't say another word."

Just then a machine gun opened fire from the direction of the elevators. John jumped on the floor and hid behind the body of his arresting officer. A bullet tore painfully into his shoulder.

Then it stopped, and John heard the old elevator start to rise. He lifted his head cautiously and saw that everyone except for one old wino was dead. The wino moaned piteously.

John rose as best he could. Wrestling with the body of the policeman, he found the keys to the handcuffs and managed to free himself. He took the gun and ammo belt just in case.

When he got to the elevator he pressed the button for down and heard a loud snapping noise and some yells, muffled, as if from behind a wall. He looked to see if someone was behind him. A policeman was moving.

"Die, pig!" he called out, firing a bullet. John smacked his lips in satisfaction at the clean hole in the man's head, the blood rushing out. Then he grew alarmed at a rushing sound and realized he would have to use the stairs.

Walking down he had to wade through festering mounds of offal. Children in the building made a habit of leaning over the rails to defecate, and anyone too tired to take the garbage downstairs just pitched it into the abyss.

Outside again, it was dark. He hailed a cab and shot the driver. Driving, he had fun running over a bicyclist and several tots who were playing a game on the sidewalk. He was going to see his former wife.

"Darling, I love you," she said when she opened the door. "Why do you have to keep pestering me?"

"I have a stomach virus, Why do you think?"

"Let's make love. I'm horny after all these years."

"No, Marlene, I'm tired of your games." He drew his gun and saw her expression, stark terror. With a blank face he pulled the trigger until it simply clicked on empty chambers. The bullets sliced through her midsection, and the body fell to the ground.

Stooping over, he grabbed into the perforations and caught hold of a section of intestine. Giving a yank he began to pull out a string of soft warm tubing that he wrapped around himself like a flower at the maypole dances. Then he danced. He danced around the room, pulling a bookcase over, smashing the glasses in the pantry, clawing at the peeling paint on the walls. He turned the television set on and watched it for a while in silence.

Then he dragged the bloody remains of his sister all around the room. He made fingerprints with the blood, decorating the refrigerator, the washer/dryer, the broken windows, the Persian rug, the books. When he was satisfied by that he drew a big knife from a drawer and severed the poor woman's head, which he attached with a string to a little toy red cart. Some more string, and he had a comfortable handle.

Out in the hallway again, he knocked on several doors before one of them opened.

A grisly sight the occupant saw: an executive-type, in a three-piece, with intestines dangling from his shoulder and neck, pulling a little red cart that bore a bloody severed head.

"Come on in. I was just heating some coffee," said the man in the door.

"No, no, I was just stopping by, I thought I might tell you the news about your best friend, he died in the Congo of yellow fever last night."

"Oh, no!" The man put his hands up to cover his face, and John saw his opportunity. He raised his knife and plunged it into the man's shoulder. Then he disemboweled the body.

"At last," he said to no one. With that he removed his clothes and painted his body with blood squeezed from the meat on the floor. "Now I can be respectable once again."

"Yes? Can I help you?" It was the cleaning lady.

"Give me that vacuum and beat it, you bitch!"

She dutifully handed over the rusting machine and left. John opened the window and tossed the vacuum out, not a second too late. The vacuum hit home, a windshield, with a loud crack, and John watched as the careening vehicle smashed into a bridge abutment under the railway crossing.

He went to the next door down the hall and kicked it in.

"Hi, honey, how was your day at work?" She gazed at him appealingly.

"Oh, okay, I guess," John grunted.

He's always grouchy after the office, she reflected.

Cost/Benefit Equations

> The price of the four freedoms is clear.
> —Djugashvili Amin Dada

> Vote for my revision of the criminal code, S-1.
> —Ted "Man O' Steel" K.

There was plenty of time to think about what I was going to do because the New Employment Plan was in the news for almost a year before the election. When the fuckhead who favored it got re-elected, I went to a few of my friends. This was where I drew the line.

We were all punks, didn't have anything worth living for. I had a job once for a few months, but some new rationing plan came through and my boss burned the place down and shot himself. I guess he wasn't making any money. None of us had jobs now except for a little dealing once in a while. I knew they'd throw in with me if the price was right.

"How much is it worth to you to take a bad risk," I said.

"What kind of risk?" they wanted to know.

"Well, I'll make sure as best I can that I take the fall if anything happens, but we're talking jail, definitely

B-mod, if they nail you. Chances are good they won't."

"Uh-uh, no way." "You kidding," they said. "Why, what you got in mind?"

"Just wait on that part. First I need to know what your price is, pick a number."

They were embarrassed. It was strange; we weren't hardcore, but here I was setting something up. "How about ten million," I said. They laughed. We all knew they'd do anything for that much if they'd be able to keep it.

"I can't go that high," I said, "but we're talking maybe two hundred thousand apiece."

"Sounds okay," they said. "Depends on how sure we are about getting paid." They pretended to take it all real cool, but they wanted me to tell them what was up.

"I'm working on it," I said. "You just keep your trap shut and stay away from me for a while."

∞ ∞ ∞

I knew I could get the money easy in just one or two nights, but I wasn't into the idea of robbing honest people. My dad used to run a liquor store till he got killed in a holdup, which soured me on that kind of scam. He hated the ban on guns, but stores got searched every once in a while by the rations people so he couldn't hide a shotgun or something under the counter.

He used to tell me about it when I was a kid. I asked

him what was all the hassle when the ban first went into effect.

"But everybody will be safer," I said.

"Maybe. Maybe safer from each other, and that's in doubt. When you need a gun, there ain't no substitute. Safety lobbies don't stand between your wife and a rapist. Besides, they won't be safer from the biggest threat, the ones who still have guns." He smiled, teasing me.

"Who? No one will have them."

"Oh yes they will. How do you think they make sure their plans for production get implemented? You know, a while back, when you could still get guns with a license, there was a class called black-powder, and you could get them without a license. You could still rob a bank with one, though. It just shows what the whole point of registration was."

"What? I don't get it."

"They're not worried about petty crimes, they're worried about the kind of weapons that would make a difference if there was some kind of resistance."

So I got it then. Freedom is a load of shit when you don't have the means to issue the final veto. Votes are made of lead.

∞ ∞ ∞

It only took about two weeks to get all the money I was going to need. I made my fundraising into a game, playing by my own rules as a point of pride.

Only people who worked for the government got hit. I followed some guys home when they got off work at the Social Security office and the Community Mental Health Center. Stuff like that. One guy who worked at the Senator's office had ten thousand on him, enough for a couple months' rent in the rent-control districts.

"I can give you what I said before," I told the guys, "for two murders apiece."

They were bowled over. "You must be crazy."

I had a lot of explaining to do. "Not murder, really," I said. "It depends on how you look at it. Think like this is a war. We're in the occupied territory." I read them the note that I wanted them to put on the bodies, the one that was taught to me by one of the underground guys I bought guns from. He and a whole bunch of people had committed suicide in jail just a day or so earlier, with help I guess.

Took about an hour to get through, but they came over. They were already sold but needed to make like they'd never be so low as to kill for money. I explained everything I had set up. I gave them the enemy locations, told them where the guns were. Then I showed them the money, and my own gun so they wouldn't get any ideas. They had to bring me proof: a finger and a wallet would be best. We were moving tonight so they wouldn't back out. It was a full moon, which was best 'cause it keeps the cops busier.

∞ ∞ ∞

I had no trouble with the first one. I had worked up my hate for a long time. The second one had a bridge game going so I had to kill all of them, which gave me more time to see the blood. I started to sweat when I changed the clip; the ones that weren't dead were screaming. I threw up outside.

It bothered me for a minute 'cause they probably didn't all work for the government. Then I figured they all knew what each other did, so if they were there they felt it was okay what the target did for a living. None of them were innocent.

∞ ∞ ∞

When I met the first guy with the money, he looked like he'd been throwing up too. I think he hated me for putting him through it, but it was him 'cause he wanted the money. He'd get over it.

"Tell me again," he said, "why we did this."

I looked around the room, an empty former laundromat at a vacant apartment house. It hit me how he felt. No one left to say it wasn't your fault, to say it's all gonna be okay in the end. Don't start that, I told myself.

"Look," I said, lighting a cigarette. "There's no end in sight. It really is a war. You know that. We only know the enemy by what they do. If they take certain jobs they got to be killed. It's like those Skinner boxes at school. Now we're doing the conditioning."

"No other way." He was looking up into the air.

Maybe they'll pick up on it, I thought, then go out and carry on the work. "We can't play around like they did when Dad was a teenager in the sixties, especially since most people his age went over to the enemy, and they think they have some divine right to run everything. They got us by the balls. We can't get riots organized. Just individuals now, doing it on their own. There's never a lot of people who care, just so long as they get their beer and TV." I paid him off, laid the money on the table when he didn't reach for it. He didn't say goodbye.

Pretty much the same with the rest. When they were all on their way I made sure to call the media so there wouldn't be a coverup, even though I knew the media always turned everything into a scare story to sell papers. I went into a bar for a beer.

I had spent a lot of time thinking about the next part. What a price, I told myself. But slaves have nothing to spend except their lives. If they want to own themselves they have to quit groveling, and it costs them everything. Might as well do as much damage as you can while you're there. When you have nothing to lose then you can afford the ideals.

Just too bad the other savages don't seem to care about who's responsible. No more underground. I finished my beer.

At the phone I called the cops to report a robbery at

the bar. Then I hid outside. When they got there I managed to hit two, but couldn't be sure they were dead. I had the wallets and the fingers. I did say I would take the fall.

∞ ∞ ∞

The president was receiving his morning briefing.

"I think we're in for trouble over the N.E.P.," said his aide. "The entire draft board was killed last night in Houston. It looks organized, there was a note. John Locke, prohibited material, sections 16 and 17 of his second treatise on civil government. They got the guy with the evidence, but he shot himself."

"Put the FBI on it. We can give the boards extra security or something..."

"I don't think that's enough, sir. It was all over the front pages, quote and all. I think people are going to get ideas. And the replacement boards in Houston have all announced their resignations."

"Draft them too! Fuck this! What's going on!" The president's temper exploded. "Close the papers then! National security!"

"I think we could get a lot of extra mileage out of rescinding the order, sir." My son is nearly draft age, the aide thought. Banning Locke was stupid.

"What are we, a nation of pussies!"

"No, sir. I think it's just that they used to have something to lose. Now it's gone. Sir." With that, the aide drew his service revolver and put a neat hole in the president's forehead.

"The third one," he thought. "I make history."

He heard a roar of applause, and he put the gun to his temple.

Two riders were approaching.

And. The. Wind. Began. To Howl.

Rodeo Week in Sheridan

It's rodeo week in Sheridan, see, and from all over the country the professional westerners come. They cause trouble as much as they can—but only in crowds, for they are timid—because they sense that they are held in contempt. Who among us is acting most like a woman, preening for hours in the morning, moving slowly throughout the day as with a heightened consciousness of appearance? Indeed, and whose women are these, that make an effort to ignore their own appearance, or intentionally degrade it so as not to upstage their men? Pompous frauds and dangerous weaklings.

Because there is this fear. Among every other man, who is most insecure about his masculinity? Which never recalls without shame his probably circle-jerks (or more extensive experiments sans the female species) around the campfire as callow youths? And from that point onward perceives every relation only in terms of dominance, because anyone who has not been mastered is likely to harbor the very doubts…"Why that dog, he probably thinks I…" yes, and if it could even occur to you, whose thought was it?

In three simple dealings with this paragon of America, for instance at work, what marks each? That the fellow who so desperately wears his special Hat and Boots and massive, crotch-centered Belt Buckle, perhaps even the gaudy rings and bracelets, so as not to be mistaken for anything else, unconscious that the very need to avoid being so identified irrevocably places him in repellent company, appears to make a habit of obnoxiousness. Some trivial act akin to snatching the pen, proffering a snide comment, must always occur one step beyond neutrality because neutrality is too close to approval. They fear everything, and hate themselves, and approval is thus anathema…it would blur the defensive lines marking the boundary of their void, their "personality." Like the grossly, immensely fat, they extend a symbolic territory to compensate for a justly-sensed lack of substance within. The coward among cowards will always be the model for bravery among savages.

Singularity

I overheard them talking. "Just look at that worm," said the snake. "Groveling in the mud, sniffing around that poor tree's roots. I swear the world is just falling apart when we have to associate with that trash."

Then there was a dog. "I just hate those uppity cats," said the dog. "They walk around with their tails in the air as if they had something to feel big about. Makes me sick."

Worms talk about snakes, too. They take careful note of the snakes unsavory character. The coyote, north and south, holds the tick in contempt. Horses sneer at the dumpy washerwoman nature of the cow. But cows don't care, nosiree, because they don't get ridden with spurs and whips.

"They have to make themselves feel important," said the mosquito of the butterfly. "But they ain't nothin'." just airheads in drag is all. They never taste blood, and they don't risk death for the proud Mosquito Empire!"

A Brief Overview of Our Activities to Date

Students tend to be well aware of the world outside and at times seem to think they are better informed by virtue of their isolation. Our PoliSci class was no exception; the twenty-nine of us took this as our starting point for a grand experiment.

"What can we do?" the teacher asked us, "to actually change the situation?" It was early in the first semester. He growled and glared around the room. "How many of you can think of a project that would within ten years revolutionize the country?"

Someone spoke up about taking part in the protests, the riots that were going on in the streets around us.

"Takes too long," the teacher said, frowning and turning toward the blackboard. He drew a triangle, labeled it HIERARCHY, and whirled back around. "Besides, what do you think happens when you take part in such resistance?" He looked around, wanting an answer.

I felt like a fish out of water. What is this? Strategies for the Revolution 101?

Someone pulled me back by answering the teacher. "If I understand," said the voice to the far left, "traditional opposition has a tendency to turn into the ruling class once it has deposed of its opposite number."

"Yes, yes!" the teacher said, brightening visibly. "Exactly." He peered out at us like an owl. "You've heard it before, of course. And seen it."

He walked to the back of the class and stood there for a moment. Some of us turned to look at him. "We're going to think the unthinkable here," he told us. "I'm going to draw it out of you. Left and Right are the sides of a coin, fighting over the spoils." He ran down to the front and drew a quick line on the board, put LEFT on one end and RIGHT on the other. "What if revolution means stepping out of the line?" he asked. Then he sat at back his desk and opened a book. "Class dismissed," he announced, looking up.

∞ ∞ ∞

That was about five years ago. Only one person has left us, lost contact; the break came during one of the pistol-practice sessions. He was a pacifist by report and although the rest if it seemed acceptable he felt that it seemed inconsistent with our ultimate goal. There was no animosity.

During the rest of the school year we studied the market and talked about a transformed world. We went on field trips, wrote pamphlets and handed them out at demonstrations. We outlined out plans, invited participation. We went to some caves for a week underground.

We camped in wilderness areas, hiked around. The habit of doing things together brought an intimacy that most of us had never known before.

What was the plan? It was simple: to put into practice the principles that would lead to the supercession of state capitalism. None of us wanted a world of wage labor, work, hierarchy, monogamy, and dream-killing boredom. We had entered the class resigned to stuff our heads full of lies that we could spit back when prompted, thus earning a piece of paper that would qualify us to take some lower-level position within the dominant institutions. But then we saw the world outside collapsing of its own dead weight, and we were torn between worry and desire: worry that those lower-level positions would be unavailable, and desire that the all-consuming flames would spread to every corner of the earth.

The teacher told us we could have what we wanted once we set our minds to it. Then he quit being a teacher and became a student along with us. He didn't know it all; he knew only where we could find some of what we needed to know. He told us he had spent ten years in academia wondering how to bring back something that was false from the beginning, a mere phenomenon urged into existence by news outlets hungry for shocks and thrills.

"When you see the cameras, it isn't real, it won't work," he told us. "It may be fun, but when it fades you're worse off. You're stuck wishing for clownhood."

∞ ∞ ∞

We did have to work a little. And we did have to fight. The fighting came later.

How long, we wondered. How many? Six years. Five hundred people. No hierarchy, which was hard at first, when we were still playing by Their rules. We contacted a number of like-minded groups, but didn't get much response. The Revolutionary Communist Party provided, what, three or four. The rest were too busy organizing, providing the shocks and thrills that the cops needed for their budget requests.

I took a job, we all took jobs, we saved money, we bought stock on Wall Street, we bought some land. In the end we were a cross-section of the working class, some of us managers here or there. Some of us washed dishes and played music in bands at night. Some of us ran heavy machinery. All the time we were talking to the people around us, explaining, getting their attention. We formed a corporation, sold stock!

Demonstrations and riots were still going on, desultory, throughout the land. But for the most part business just kept going. The headlines screamed about this or that, as they had to. The revolutionary developments they trumpeted about had about as much effect on your life as the moons on Saturn. Some, but not much. We had discussions with people who wanted to help them fight, help them provide more news. Some of them came over to us.

∞ ∞ ∞

Our first major move had to be a good one, to establish credibility. We were cold and calculating. We spent a lot of time figuring, playing with numbers. Sometimes it got to be a drag. We had to pay attention to PR, so we started with food. We bought farms and staffed them, and then we announced: FREE FOOD! We opened a stand near the city and just gave it away, handing out pamphlets about our project and talking to people.

Then the regulators came in, tried to shut us down. We got on the PA near the stand and identified the regulators, asked the people milling around how they felt about it.

"But the grocery stores are going to have problems," the men told us.

"So?" I said. With the microphone, I asked for help. "How many of you would like to help us drive off these people who want to make you pay for something that we want to give away?"

The regulators left. But we knew they'd be back when we moved on to bigger things.

We managed to keep the free food going for a while. We poured more of our capital into it than we had expected, came squeaky-close to crippling ourselves. In the end we were doing underhanded things like paying off truckers with loads for the stores, and giving them new identities.

But our plans worked out. One of the stores in the

town that had been operating on a thin margin announced that it would go out of business. We bought them out. We decided to simply slash prices rather than give it all away. We had volunteers so we didn't need to pay for the help. That way we could stay in business long enough to weaken the other stores. The cashiers didn't need to be well trained because they didn't put up of much of a hassle if people were short.

All this generated a lot of attention, and more people bought stock in our company, enabling us to buy more in other companies. Our original group was now spread far and wide, and we only got together once a year or so. We kept our hands in other operations, saving, readying ourselves for the next coup.

Meanwhile other stores were going out of business, and we bought them, too, slashing prices but staying open so no other competitors could move in. We undercut them all, but we had to make sure to stock the shelves because if the food ran out we'd go bust.

"They're crazy!" screamed Wall Street. "What are they up to?"

"We love them!" replied the people. "We don't care!"

When we bought controlling interest in a steel refinery they began to get the picture, and we didn't mind that our buyers were other large corporations. Investment brokers started jumping out of windows when our buyers refused to miss the deal we offered on steel products.

∞ ∞ ∞

It was all voluntary trade and we didn't worry about profits so much so we could afford to cut prices to the maximum. We had workers who would work for free a'la Ernest Free Man, and we gave them food or land, or money if they really needed it. They could do whatever they wanted, but they all realized that if they went into competition with us we'd undercut them ruthlessly.

Of course, we had to deal with people from the government. The other capitalists were running scared, asking for the regulators to protect their position.

But we had printing presses, too, and we had voters who didn't like to think that free food was going to be outlawed by certain candidates.

At last word 7Exxon was announcing default on its debts. *Forbes* and *Fortune* went under long ago. And Lou Grant, I heard, was seriously considering our bid to manage *The Wall Street Journal*. We started giving away gasoline about a year ago.

The Devil's Day Off

During one of those hundred-year-long days that Satan will on occasion spend simply savoring the boundless opportunity this planet offers to rebels like himself it happened that he crossed paths with a contingent of roving Heaven's Angels. These were troublemakers of the worst sort, raze-the-village-to-save-it types, a bizarre little army created by god to throw a monkey wrench into the works as a randomizing element. They were the holy spirits sent out to raise hell and drive people away from Satan.

Now on this day, hoping to relax and enjoy the scenery, Satan had decided not to bring along those devilish high-tech gadgets that keep him linked to the databanks in Hell. Thus he was stranded much like Scotty or Captain Kirk, without the communication devices that enabled them to beam up or to take x-ray photos, alone on an alien planet full of marauding hooligans who had no sense of law or decency.

"What are you fellows doing out today?" said Satan, swallowing.

The tallest had a gleam in his eye. He could tell Satan

had no access to the databanks. "Oh, we've been out in the service of the Lord," he said, chuckling. "We raped and pillaged a little, then we torched New York with an A-Bomb. All the humans are in a tizzy trying to figure out who or why." All the Heaven's Angels snickered.

"You faggots!" yelled Satan, "What about their lives, all those millions of minutes and hours they could have spent on something they wanted to spend them on!" He was enraged.

All the Heaven's Angels let out hoarse guffaws. "Oh, isn't he Mister Morality today," "Listen to this," "The lord moves in mysterious ways," and so on.

Now Satan hadn't left his powers at home; it was just that he didn't have the information he might need to make the best of it. This last outburst by the Heaven's Angels so incensed him that he exploded and threw a huge fireball at the group. Their earthly bodies were burnt to a crisp within nanoseconds. Since they feel the same pleasure and pain that we do when they take on earthly guises, they were not amused to melt like wax near the fireplace and go through combustion and so on. In fact they were hopping mad.

Satan knew he had blown it the instant the fire hit them. Now they were free spirits, with even more power than before because they were disincorporated and no longer restricted. Satan couldn't even tell where they were.

Just then his skull cracked open like an egg and all

his earthly limbs were torn from his body. "Fuck!" he thought. "You bastards!" A pack of dogs appeared and ate all the flesh off the bones. Then all was quiet.

Later still he gathered the bones together with spirit powers or whatever and used them to pack raw dirt close around the bones themselves, which he then breathed life into. He set out again down the road, but he had a raging headache from all the esters and effluents from the dirty water which he had to use for blood. When he pissed it out he was dehydrated and hungry and had those aches and pains generally associated with metempsychosis from scratch.

Soon he came to a house. As he walked up the path past the daisies and magnolias he wondered what he would say to the people inside. He arrived at the doorstep and knocked.

"Yes," cried a woman inside, "who is it?"

Satan sighed to himself. "I'm going to have to be straight with you, ma'am. I'm the devil. I just want a glass of water."

He heard her laughing on the way to the door, then saying, "Oh, Sammy, how you tease me so," while she opened the door. Her first glance produced a scream of fright, followed by a trance spouting fit of speaking in tongues. He knew what she was saying because he knew all tongues. Most of it was true gibberish, but the point of it all was that she was a devout Christian.

The sound, of course, hurt his ears, so he left, figuring

he wouldn't likely get a glass of water when she came to.

At the next house he came to he knocked again. A young Korean Buddhist woman came to the door. She giggled when she saw who it was. "Can I help you?"

"Yes, ma'am, I'd like a glass of water."

"Come on in, I just happen to have some nice Kimchi on hand."

Kimchi is a hot food so Satan thought it was excellent. He hates the bland mush they put out in fast food places even though he started them in the first place. He stayed a long time, even drinking a small glass of whisky, and talked to the young lady about the trials and tribulations of raising active children.

"How are they doing in school?" he asked.

"The teachers are having a hell of a time," she said, and they both laughed.

"Aren't you afraid of me?" he asked after a while, wondering.

"Why? You don't have any jurisdiction!" They both laughed again, and slapped their knees.

When the children got off the school bus their mother asked Satan if he would mind playing with them for a while so she could take a nap. He was pleased to and spent a few hours teaching them about Dungeons & Dragons. As a special favor he touched them all on the forehead and blessed them with superior intelligence so they would do well in the world when they grew up and so that the pains wouldn't hurt so badly.

Then he had dinner with the entire family, and talked business with the man of the house, who was very interested in the doings up above. Satan gave him some important tips about the market and told him which stocks were going to rise within the next few months. Everyone was thrilled to have such an important guest and felt honored to render him some kind of humble service.

Finally Satan told them he had to go and attend to some important matters that had cropped up earlier in the day when he ran into some old buddies. The children were disappointed.

"Oh, Mr. Devil," they said, "we don't want you to go back to the terrible places. Stay and play with us."

"No, no, kiddies, I have to go. You'll find plenty to do without me." Then he turned to the young couple once again and told them he would grant them one major boon without any small print.

Both laughed shyly. "Oh, no, you don't have to," they said.

"Whatever you wish," he replied. Then he took his leave, and he didn't forget to tilt their luck plane in the direction of good before leaving the area. At least their house would never get struck by a tree limb or burn down or anything.

On judgment day, sometime after, the first lady was turned away at the gates of Heaven. "Remember when Satan came to ask you for a drink of water?" Jesus asked her. "You turned him down! That wasn't very Christian of you!"

The Korean family wasn't there at all. There was no jurisdiction.

Revisionist History for Children

In the mountains around Tibet there is hidden an ancient monastery with a few wise monks. For centuries these monks, some of whom are actually over five hundred years old, have sturdily kept the promise they made to the Master of the Universe, which was to make sure that at all times, somewhere in the world, at least five people would be thinking the name of god at all times.

The Master of the Universe is busy somewhere else for a long, long time, and he can't be around to watch and make sure that all is going well in his domain. Therefore, he asked the monks to keep alive the memory of the king, even when everyone has died and forgotten it, even when all the rocks that knew him had been ground into powder and melted. If he is forgotten then the world will vanish, and all that will be left is pain for the spirits of all the things that were.

A little while ago one of the monks, who had been the best student In his youth four hundred years ago, fell asleep during his prayer period, and a terrible earthquake happened, because the seams of the world of

Things began to unravel just a little bit. This happened a few more times and once two monks happened to be asleep for a whole ten minutes and because of this a giant bomb fell very close to the monks on cities in Japan. Much weeping went on, and only a few Masters in Japan were there who knew about the few monks who kept the world alive. When one burned up in Vietnam his spirit sent out such a cry of anguish that it woke up a sleeping monk, but this wasn't enough because, of course, the optimum number of monks has never been calculated.

Some say that if there were one hundred monks who studied the ancient wisdom all praying and thinking of god's name all the time, there would never be a war. If there were two hundred monks, then everyone would return to childhood and be happy, and the birds would bring our food to us, and the lions would guard us against the bears, and the wolves would make friends with the days again and they would keep an eye on the crops for the birds, so that the pheasants would not be too greedy and eat too much.

But with only five monks, the world is very sorry all the time since it is just right on the edge of dissolving. And there can't be more than five because some of them have to watch the spirits of the night, and others must tend the snow gardens so that Beauty won't go away from the Earth. They have many other very important tasks to attend to. Some of them are busy trying to rediscover the One Word that will bring god back if it is spoken aloud. This word was forgotten because only the Wisest Monk knew it. When god told it to him before he went away, he said, "This is the most important word I have created, and you must never use it unless it is almost too late. Don't even tell anyone, even if you die, because if you tell them, it will be spoken aloud, and its power will be unleashed, never to be assembled again. Bad things will happen if it isn't used when it is time for it to be used, because the Guard at the Door of Meaning will know if I am needed, and if I am not he will send the word into another part of the building, where it will revive many strange and terrible things. If you die, the monks will remember the word when it is time to use it, even though they may not realize they have found it, and might not use it."

The Wisest Monk died one day and forgot the word to call god, but the monks have many, many other tasks to fulfill. Each day they must refill the twenty pails and water the twenty trees so that no drought will ever happen, but they are shorthanded and only have enough strength to get to some of them. One tree died and all the monks wept because now there will always be a drought somewhere in the world. The monks also must plant seeds of sand in the floor of the monastery so that the stars will not fall out of the sky, and sometimes when they can't plant enough on rainy nights, stars begin to fall onto the earth. You can see them falling, and they are so angry about falling that if they catch you, they'll burn a hole right through.

The monks are very busy. Some of them are frightened sometimes, because they know how much they must do, and each day they must caress the rock of sadness with the finest silk cloths, to wash away the sadness. If they have time, they can wash away enough to make people happy without any reason, but every day more sadness enters the world and the first people to feel it are the monks. They are so busy that many days, they postpone tending the rock of sadness until it becomes almost unbearable, and this is why so many people are sad, because the monks have so much to do.

In this way some of the monks have died before their time (which is measured on the String of Life, another tale), because they feel the sadness the most, and they try to hold it back so that it won't go and spread to other people. They can hold more than one hundred men, but they are a small wall against the oceans of tears that will pour, and sometimes they get so much that they run and fall over the cliffs. Even worse, the spirits of the night wrestle with the monks while they sleep, and if the monks don't win, some of the spirits escape into the day and make mischief on the Earth. Once when the monks were attacked by many many spirits, all of them escaped and caused a great plague in Europe. It is these spirits that make the monks fall asleep when they should be thinking of god's name, but it can't be helped.

The monks have so much power that if they touch anything, it will be able to heal any disease, but they can't use their power this way very much because then they wouldn't have it to use against the infinite enemies of life.

More Revisionism

Our tribe knows the story of the one who found the door by accident. When the boy was born the wise men looked in his face for signs of what his name would be, and they were troubled for the signs showed that the boy would grow to be a student of the elders but that they would curse him and he would have his vengeance. Their curse would be a mistake. They named him, Forgive Us.

Forgive Us was healthy like all the boys in our tribe and grew quickly. Before long he stayed with the elders except during the period of the hunt, and he learned their secrets slowly. They said he was a good student, but a distracted one, because his mind would wander during lessons and he would come back or leap forward to questions about different matters. Once he asked the elders how they came to be in the first place and no one knew the answer; they shook their heads and reminded themselves of what the child's face had said.

Then came the time when Forgive Us had to learn an important secret about the door to the other world. The elders brought him to the cave along with some other students, where many prayers were said and sacrifices were made. Each student was given time with the chief who would show how to use the Key to the door. Forgive Us was the last student to try the Key that day and even though he knew that most students would have no success at first, he became angry.

"I can't do it!" he said, and left.

Outside the cave an elder caught up with him and told him not to worry, but Forgive Us could not be cheered. That night a bear stole into the cave and rumbled around like bears will do, and it just so happened that the bear broke the Key. Of course when it was discovered the elders grew deeply angry since now they had no way to contact the spirits of the hunt. "Who would do such a thing?" they asked each other, and they thought of only one person: Forgive Us.

The next day the elders gathered and Forgive Us was cursed and he had to leave the tribe. Everybody watched him and he didn't say anything but just turned to go and walked away. After that it wasn't long before people forgot.

But Forgive Us didn't because he had to walk the whole way across the land and he was hungry most of the time, and the rocks were cold to sleep on, and the little creatures bit him in the air. Long after he began to walk he was captured by another tribe and they spoke harshly as if their mouths hated the words they spoke, and they made him tend the fire, which is a woman's job, and he could only have scraps left over from when the rest were done eating. All the people in the tribe spit on him and talked about how nice he would be for dinner later when the air grew cold and food was scarce.

"Ha, he likes the trees!" said some. "Let's tie him to the tree and set it on fire!"

"No," said some others, "wouldn't it be more fun to pin him to the tree with a spear? Ha ha!"

Some grumbled and suggested that they cut his head off because it was a burden to keep him around.

Just when the hunters were about to reach a decision Forgive Us looked on the ground and saw something which he reached for, and he vanished from the eyes of the hunters because it was the handle to the door outside, which can be turned by anyone with the Key, from afar, but only people who find it can turn it without the Key.

Forgive Us was standing on the edge of a cliff and the Eagle spoke to him, saying, "You are far from home," where berries are being picked. In the baskets were many berries and Forgive Us was inside one of them and tasted it and then turned the handle again and he was in the wind. In the wind he found grains and tears of the sky but they said nothing, and Forgive Us went up as high as he could until his skin burned away from the heat of the sun, and his bones crumbled into dust, but they kept going with him.

He flew and flew and all the time he felt as if he was

burning even though his body was already burned up. He knew he was cursed so he didn't complain to himself.

Then Forgive Us found the heart of the universe and saw where all the spirits gather nearby, and he still had his hand on the handle of the door so he turned it and then he grabbed onto the heart of the universe! It was a little thing and when Forgive Us squeezed it he was tormented by the screams of a thousand suns who felt pain. None of the spirits could come near him while he held the heart, and he sat back and thought, and when he squeezed again the elders realized that history is a nightmare from which we wake to find ourselves in a torture chamber. For glittering things. Came into the hands of the tribes. And lived to move but were dead. The elders called his name.

Winning Hearts & Minds

I don't know what my rank is, or even if I have one for that matter. There isn't anyone to give them out as far as I can tell. I'm not in an army I guess, but whenever I run across people with guns they seem to be fighting, and they try to capture me and anyone else that I'm with.

Most people don't seem to think of themselves as combatants, they don't believe in the war. I tried to explain it to one guy that I was supposed to recruit (that's my job, recruiting, but not on any orders from above because there isn't any above) and I said, "There aren't any neutrals."

This turned him off. "That's what they all say when they want to get you involved," he told me.

"Well, I was wrong then," I said. I knew it was a lost cause but I kept on, at least because I had to figure out just what I meant. "There are people who don't fight, who give up, they submit by default, and they think they're neutral, but there aren't any people who don't fall on one side or another. You can choose to submit, and it doesn't mean you deserve what you get because maybe your assessment was correct, that you couldn't win here and now. The ones who say you deserve what you get if you don't fight are the enemy, because then if they get power they'll do what they please and say you deserve it because you didn't fight. You don't have to fight, but you have to if you want something different."

I think he understood, but wanted to wait and see. Most people don't want to throw in with suicide squads when the whole point is to live better. But we need more people if it is going to be anything but a suicide squad.

I've seen every sort of action, from full-scale bombardment to infiltration, from capturing the enemy to being captured. I spent a long time in an enemy concentration camp, but I escaped because it was under the direction of people who thought they were running a rehabilitation camp for people on their side who had simply lost track. It was far from the center of the fighting, in a secure position, and the directors knew they were in such a solid position that they didn't need to go overboard with the security measures. I kept going after that. Before I was captured I didn't even know that I was fighting, or that there was a war going on. I've never seen any kind of base camp for our side in all this time. There's no headquarters, no capitol, no place to regroup. I think we've been scattered, as if the war was won long ago by the enemy, and everyone forgot about it except when the abuses became extreme, or when they found some old books about it that hadn't been burned. I wonder about it sometimes, though, because I know where all this ammo is stored, and there are little groups here and there who talk about the major offensive that's just around the corner. I've seen the ammo dumps, there are thousands of huge tanks and planes and guns and all, and it's all being turned out by no more than a dozen men and women on these massive machines. A few stragglers would drift in like myself every day or so and take what they could use, then leave. They all had stories about the fighting, about their local strategies, goals and all, and we shared info and codes and meeting places, and signed up to go help here or there. But there were never enough of us there at one time to make use of the tanks and planes.

I went with one group and stood with them against a full-scale invasion. All we had were machine guns, and we couldn't hold up so we were dispersed, and I ended up in another place where the people didn't even notice the enemy. "Look, over there, it's a tank and a bunch of army personnel."

"Tank? So?"

"But they take your food, they kill you."

"We give it to them because they need it to protect us. Besides, they only kill us when we don't give it to them."

"What if you starve?"

"If we get hungry we can always join their army, then we have all we need."

"Wouldn't it be simpler to just get rid of them and keep your food? You obviously don't get enough to eat."

The one I was talking to was a mother with a child; the child had a bloated stomach, classic symptoms.

"But if we got rid of them, why, then there wouldn't be anybody to make sure we tended our fields!"

Sometimes there are people living in an area where the invasion hasn't taken place, or where the army is weak and could be thrown off with a minimal effort. I establish some contacts, then scout out ahead with a few people. Others get sent back to the warehouses to bring back the weapons we'll need. Hardly anyone goes, though.

"But the tanks are coming!"

"Tanks? Show us these tanks, we don't see any."

The new contacts are exasperated along with me, but we don't do any good, and the tanks roll in, usually to the sound of a parade.

Then there are the few who know about the tanks, the ones who say the only way to resist is to paint the tanks at night, make them look stupid. But the food still gets taken at gunpoint.

In all of this one group is the most frustrating, and one is most able to bring on fits of despair. The first ones are the people who have seen the tanks, who know that the food gets stolen, but who don't believe in our warehouses.

"You don't have enough weapons to stop them," they say, "so just go away and stop bothering us."

"But I've seen them! All we need is people to staff these weapons, then we can win!"

"Humbug, you're just giving us false hopes."

"Free for the taking, tons and tons, bombs that will smash a hundred enemy tanks!"

They snicker and still refuse to believe.

The worst of all, I suppose, the ones that bring on despair, are the people in the enclaves that resist us. They hate the enemy, but they fight us too, even when they know the enemy is on the way and that we would help. They think they're strong when they can beat off a single corporal, a scout, armed with one beat up gun, with their pitchforks and hoes. They're all proud of their accomplishments, crowing at night, but they haven't seen the tanks. "We have enough weapons, leave us alone," they laugh.

"You'll be sorry," I reply, not a very good recruiter after all.

"Anyway, if we lose we'll join up with the invaders and then we'll be okay."

Well, maybe so. But I've seen those tanks, the ones they were too afraid to check out, and I've seen the warehouses, and I've seen the increasing number of people who go to the warehouses. By now the warehouses are secure against invasion, even if they can't launch an offensive. And nobody likes a mercenary; in the end, no matter which side wins, the mercenary loses.

Melpomene's Little Sister Georgene

Melpomene had a little sister who was very pretty and delicate and she was bitter as nutmeg because when the gods were creating her a prankster poured in too much of the spice. Melpomene's little sister wasn't destined to be talented or influential like the other muses so one day she fell in with a few mortals and left with them to go on adventures.

She was of course bitterly unhappy that day, but no more so than on any other day of being in the company of brilliant, busy people and gods. None of these had ever intentionally made her feel bad over the fact that she was the victim of a trick; after all, they were wise and friendly most of the time unless they had gotten into the ambrosia. But still, you know how it is. Lately she had begun to wonder what the more important gods were planning for her, since a few times when they visited they paid close attention to her and whispered to each other about what should be done with the mistake.

So while she was bitterly unhappy among the mortals, who always thought they were on adventures no matter how miserable they were, it was probably better to escape. The world of mortals was new to her, however, and she was kept preoccupied with the dangers of her flight and worried about what the gods would do if they found her. After all, she possessed important secrets that anyone would pick up hanging around in such company. Anyway, being distracted by the peculiarities and difficulties of the mortals, she never found time to stop and gather her wits about her.

It wasn't long before she forgot the secrets she had learned, and even that she had ever known them. She couldn't speak with the mortals about most of her experiences, since these were beyond their comprehension, and she made her way through the land of the mortals in a haphazard fashion with no clue as to what angles were best for her when negotiating with people, or deciding on courses of action. Many of the lessons that mortals learn at a young age were ones that she had to learn by making mistakes, or weren't learned at all. For instance most mortals take for granted that the stranger is an enemy and don't take it hard when they're treated shabbily by established groups. But when she tried to go among the young mortals at a school, nobody could tell for sure what it was but they sensed something different about her and because of this she could never get close to any of them. They were distant and suspicious and even cruel; like most of the mortals they are aware that they must die, which makes them jealous of their time and by extension, everything else.

Another time she was lured into a trap by one of the mortals, who fell in love with her. She was very pretty after all, and always had the bitter and subtle power of the spice in her, which could easily drive the mortals mad with desire. Anyone who was made by the gods always has a touch of magic about them even if it isn't too strong and when she wasn't concentrating sometimes, if people walked by her or stood close on the bus, they would get the same feeling as if they heard the blues, or if they were former junkies they would feel the warmth grow in their stomachs and maybe fall, without ever realizing what had reminded them of pain in desire, foreknowledge of hopelessness, like an elegant chess combination which must be played even if it leads to loss. Anyway, she allowed this mortal to think he was conducting a great love affair with a mysterious girl and it wasn't long before she gave birth to a child.

This mortal man could never figure it out, though, why she was distant, and he wasn't even one of the better mortals. Deeply troubled by their fate, they usually spend their time feeling sorry for themselves, which is understandable but no excuse. Naturally she was bitter being surrounded by people who were blind to hidden qualities as a result of having concluded that noble undertakings all end in failure. She was unable to share their particular sorrow, seeing as how she was born in between the two worlds. People like that can never feel at home in the world unless they make some kind of special effort that is almost guaranteed to use them up and by then it doesn't matter. Even her baby was somewhat of a mystery to her, since it was mostly a mortal child.

Bitter isn't the opposite of sweet. This is because both are sharp in their pure states. Bitter is a complete spirit in itself that was one of the essences put into the universe by the gods in order to prevent blandness from allying itself with sweet against sour, and of course this means that the opposite of bitter is dull. Everywhere that Melpomene's little sister looked, she saw that the mortals relied on the use of bland to console themselves, and having so many thoughts bothering her she mistakenly came to believe that, like them, she needed to wash herself in the bland essences, to balance the bitter which always made her feel as if she were being consumed. This was the kind of error most people make, to think relief comes from mixing together the opposites. What needed to be done was to get the opposite out so as to purify the stronger element, and then find examples of different crystalline perfection and dance with them, not melt together and grow dim. These are god secrets that were stolen long ago, but we mortals are always trying to steal from the gods and nobody thinks anything of it. We're a rum crew and it's a rum show and if we play our cards right we can enjoy some of the benefits of the gods without paying too much penalty.

Melpomene's little sister never had a Name except

the one the mortals used on her, Georgene, and that's why she was so lonely. A name can be anything, but a Name is something else entirely. As time went on, she realized that the mortals would be cruel to her without ever knowing why they had to. But she didn't know why either, and the truth was that they can't share their names like the gods can unless they've taken great risks and stolen a number of important secrets from you-know-who. They can't share their little names that mean only very small amounts of meaning; there isn't enough to go around. It's the mortal way to be mean with those who have less, so as to remind the one with more that he has something; their consciousness is very reliant on contrast, like the lower animals. They gang up, and they'll be cruel until people die of it, so Melpomene's little sister should have been more careful when she was around them, but you know how it goes.

One time she met a mortal man who was very curious, seeing as how he made a profession out of certain dangerous smuggling missions and raids against certain parties who have powers they uncharitably withhold from us if you catch the drift, and they talked for a long time until it was late, but she wouldn't let him do the honorable thing and walk her home. He sat for a while and shook his head and thought about a few other pretty girls he had known who had to walk home at night.

Digressions

Describing his courtroom ordeals and conferences with the law Matt always permitted me to cultivate an image of his X-wife as the possessor of a cruel intelligence... a spider at the center of a web of policemen, child support truancy officers, AFDC and family counseling, women's center or crisis line struts in the tenuous but solid framework of a trap. Sorting out the players in the puzzle beside being tedious was a touch beyond me and this probably as a result of getting my information secondhand from a fellow who could not honestly be said to have sorted it out himself. I never did get straight whether he left her or the other way around or even what kind of conflicts could occur between them; but this is nothing new now that I recall Tom has an X-wife too and he's very subdued when you could imagine that he was dashing once. Tom reads Epictetus these days and pays on time, gets the kid on random weekends by court order in the plan for the bureaucratization of all social relations, and I've seen her, cute one next to loving dad. Matt is broke and glad they can't squeeze an empty shell, to the extent that I sometimes wonder if his habit of neglecting to bathe isn't part of a conscious program, but when I saw his boy who must be four now and doesn't talk very much my opinions changed little.

Only a little though, since we don't have much room for your Christian liberal brand of pity which has all manner of unsavory precursors. There are essays about the feminization of poverty that amount to about as much as any caucus polemic ever did, but I've spent hours encoding the Question in a vain attempt to like *intuit* the nature of this virus. From one angle I look at the number of widows through history as a percentage of population, and wars take up the slack I guess when we ask ourselves have there ever been sizeable numbers of mom, singular. I recall the objection to Spock which runs: your error is to pretend you're going to be able to sculpt these cussed blanks in the first place. Let them alone and give them a few items they ask for and you'll be doing more than what has kept the species alive so far. Then I dismiss it with a nod to the perspective faction which asks whether things look thick or not when you're in the middle of them.

Dave and Ken and I had to use plan B for drinking which was to stop by Donna's, once we had rejected park for Law and Cold reasons.

"She has MTV," they pointed out, and so we showed up each carrying a fifth of Beam and a six of beer. Knock, knock.

"This is Donna, Mark's X-wife," Ken introduced.

"Look at me I have curlers in my hair!" she announced. I saw an immensely fat woman. In a spare set of rooms, the reconstituted-generic domicile which always looks upscale when fresh. On the inside of the bathroom door was a schedule for daily updating with a box for each possible time when the boy had gone potty, along with some sheet on which I caught the word reinforcement.

Later, Ken hit my arm. "Look, the Pretenders," he said.

"There is a resemblance isn't there."

"Not here," he told me with an obscene grin.

"Motherfucker," I said.

I recall that we went out later and got two more fifths and shouted about jobs on the way home.

Drifting in One Spot — 1

Now this guy Doug always seemed to think that no statement could be made that did not deserve a rejoinder by Him in this world-as-a-stage drive to keep the spotlight from swinging around too much, but we forgave him half the time because as Voltaire said, it's okay to talk about yourself provided you can be entertaining. But if Doug talked too much, Ben Jordan talks too little, and they both talk just a tad too loud. It's a mercy neither of them ever got an idea that they should be telling the rest of us how to live because they both possess this mighty Word Power, the kind that can swivel every head in a coffee shop without even trying. If they learned a few opinions about anything of consequence they could have been revival-tent preachers, Chautauqua politicians, rock stars or coaches with heart conditions.

So anyway Doug took off for Kansas City a little while back; the night before the final deadline him and me and Brent polished off a fifth of Yukon Jack and had a terrible argument about everything from Tits as opposed to Ass and on down to nuclear physics and the gold standard, with plenty in between, including two lightning chess games the first of which I lost miserably and second of which I kicked butt. The final terrible conflict raged over Perkins Cake and Steak vs. some bullshit snack shop and it woke up the neighbors; all the way down to Perkins Doug was doing his wild Caledonian Pict shtick in the street and nearly getting killed screaming Nazi slogans: "*Arbeit Macht Frei!*" for the benefit of some Ford Truck spiritual essence. He ate a book of matches, staple and all, with his bowl of chili.

In the morning I decided it was vitamin day, recalling back when I was in Ansonia living with drunk Vets who would retell gook murder exploits at every party. I was in the height of my phase of health cult membership and couldn't get these fools to eat a hundred different pills in the morning. But one night I told the assembled group I had this weird drug to turn them red as lobsters and make them feel like they had sunburns with wood straitjackets on.

"Ah, ah, what is this," they told me.

"Yeah," I said, "and it comes on in fifteen minutes, it lasts fifteen minutes, you get this total rush, then it's gone! Like that!" I got the bottle, Niacin 250 milligram hits, and just started pushing it at everybody. Someone broke and then they all had to be macho and go through the initiation, so about ten minutes later they're going, "Ah, this is just some candy-ass vitamin he tricked us into taking," but they began to sit up and have wild looks on their faces. They tried the shower but it felt like getting stroked with a wire brush, and I told them to drink a bunch of water to make it flush out.

They threatened to kill me after inquiring again about how long it lasted when I said, "Oh, two, maybe three hours…" and started laughing: this was a worse trick, to give them this drug for pain and agony, saying it wouldn't last too long.

But after that this guy Bob started to believe in the Power of the Pills, and he was all worried about his tremor after being drunk about four years. I said it was all just magnesium and the B stuff being depleted, and one morning he was hung over and wanted something, "don't you have anything that will help… "

"Yeah, sure thing!" says I, the happy recruiter. I poured out about twenty capsules and pills and gelatin oil balls going through the routine to make it look as bad as possible like This Is Only The Beginning, and he told me to change my name to Elvis, but later in the day when he came home he was convinced I'd given him acid: the tremor was gone, he was tripping all day with clear thoughts and pure Mental Power! and give me another dose right now! After four years of beer and Burger King food you can bet that it will have an effect. I was the Doctor.

I sent Doug off with a similar treatment, since hitchhiking throughout cold empty spaces toward your brother's whore of an X-wife plus being broke and with no drugs can only be helped by miraculous healing chemicals circulating through starved brain cells and liver sores to make for a chipper, bright and alert confident feeling of being the Master of your Destiny, that kind of thing. You can talk to truckers about anything and not feel as if they have a knife hidden away for when the moment comes to perform terrible acts of sex murder.

Now he's gone for a while and Ben Jordan is still here, so either way we have a loud mouthed son of a bitch wandering around saying stupid things for effect. Ben's the town's biggest junkie now that Ed Gardner is dead, being so utterly wasted on pure V.A. Hospital drugs that he doesn't know what year it is. My favorite thing about him is when he'll be sitting alone or pacing in the lobby, and cut loose laughing. I know that feeling and sometimes I'll start laughing too, and he looks at you like he just communicated the joke by silent inter-mind drug magic. It is only an event that can happen to the most self-contained of characters, and I guess it is disturbing to bystanders who fear self-starting mechanisms of any kind, but it is harmless power and very tricky. I will mark one good mark for any stranger that I see who will get hysterical just by thinking about something, and try to get to know him, even if he has bizarre gestures or old clothes.

Drifting in One Spot — 2

Trailways pulls in from all points beyond at about 1:30 a.m. most nights and aside from the cops or the taxi drivers I'm the first one to interview the folks who decided to reach the end of the line in Sheridan. The summer is busy and almost every morning a few drunks stumble in or maybe hippies with backpacks. Indians and Mexicans don't ask me for a room, just where the campground is, but the hippies can surprise you by pulling American Express cards out of their plastic velcro RRRIPPP wallets, slavophilic, cheap.

In fact Trailways is how I arrived here, on the late bus (from Casper) and I hopped off already knowing where the Center was, and I spent my last bucks on the room for a night complete with televised 1951 spy movie full of alienation themes that must be scheduled to air whenever drifters settle in for the night somewhere. Now I have the job of the fellow who sold me that room, and he's glad he has another one, I bet.

So the winters are slower and the drunks will tend to ask if they can stay inside the lobby and warm up but if it seems like they mean to catch a bus-station style catnap I explain that I'm not running a Reagan Ranch. Right around last Christmas about a few days beforehand I was surprised by an unattractive girl of maybe 15 or less who pops in Sunday night off the bus and of course even with the lust in my heart I had leftover charitable impulses enough to offer coffee.

It was not long to establish that young miss was if not a junkie then at least a chipper and probably carrying AIDS or worse, if you stay up all night developing your models the way Freud did by studying only the sick at heart and then meet a hallucinating bimbo with swollen glands and respiratory problems from Kansas on her way to Billings to stay with a guy she knew there over Christmas. Lust dies and To While Away Ye Hours I asked did she play Chess only to find that while the answer is to affirm, distractions precluded absorption of the lesson about how the Knight moved.

To wrap it up I allowed her to sit and doze and when off duty bought breakfast because it was fun to know that all the dumpy daughters-of-Boss with eye on me now also have eye on messy girl at table from nowhere. Then we hit on Doug's door at the Edwards and he doled out a few pink hearts to himself and those around him so that high gear would have company but we split up, babe to Billings we presume and we for Morning Scotch and bull session.

All by way of introducing Trailways girl. Anyway, some months ago or some time I don't recall we had another god damned wedding party for lowlifes who still believe if you spend money on it maybe it will stick. Coming on duty that night meant dealing with smashing-table, beer-on-floor pouring types in the back room so I paged Security to help. There were even some grim swarthy boys from South de Border, with even-odds that the late people leftover were only most distant friends of the groom and good luck to him if the bride.

We kicked out the assholes and the creeps after time but we got a rack o' shit in return and I didn't fail to make note of how in future I'll be disinclined to do favors for men named MacDonald in this county. Later on while I was rereading Araby, what to my trembling eyes should appear but the babe of Trailways who many months back waltzed in on deathbed! She was accompanied by the tricked-up Trina, and it was meet and right that this one not be called: Katrina. Pout, makeup, swollen lip protrudes in challenge, sullen. Not at all cute but ready and that's enough.

They sit there and yeah, it's February that's right, because Babe (name forgotten if ever known) asks, — Got any hearts candy?

— H'm, says I. No—o. Now wait a second.

I run back to room where wedding was and return with a plateful of what just happens to be candies in the shape of hearts for Valentine wedding.

— Oh, they groan.

— What, go ahead, have some. They roll their eyes to each other and I grin and then I groan myself. The phone rings.

— Hello, Sheridan Center, etc.

— Yes, I left my pocketbook, would you look.

The wedding party, I think. — Certainly yes, be right back, I tell her.

In back room right there is pocketbook among bottles on floor and contents strewn. Hair curler, baggie of weed, wallet, what-else. Stuff all into bag and run front. On phone say, YES WE HAVE IT AND YOU MAY STOP BY TO PICK IT UP.

— It's very important thank you.

Now is time to snap my fingers and grab attention of Trina plus.

— Now, I ask them. If you were to be finders and others were weepers on the case of the bag of weed, would you regard it is immoral to engage in redistribution to help friends when they are down?

Both rush forward when the critical three words of communion are told up, and saying — yes yes, give it to me, give it. So Ah reaches in quicklike and out, and in a trice they is gone.

Now it wasn't even very long afterward that a nice young lady obviously from out the college drove up and smiled and asked where is the pocketbook. I have to say I didn't swallow hard or anything. With a glance inside she snaps it shut.

— Thanks very much, sir, thanks, she says and is gone.

Nor sight nor sound of the three has been back to electrify me.

Family Notes — 1/8/84

The baby was flown down to Denver last night because it was two months early and having trouble breathing, maybe some other early baby flaws. Jo I heard was talking about something or other unrelated so I assume she is in fine health if not home already, and Ed called last night for a five o'clock wake-up call which means he's going to work. They just got married last month and the whole coffee bar was there, and then for Christmas Jo, who is very businesslike and becoming motherly, made up little boxes of cookies and cake for even the irregulars.

What makes us all nervous is that we all knew very quietly that Jo had crazy operations and uterine problems and could never have a baby, and so even the most fastidious of people were tolerant when they began living together. Like the ones who can never walk or look pretty; they can compensate by doing something others might worry about. But then she went to the doctor and it was fun waiting all those months before her father even began to wonder about the bulge.

Everybody concurs that Jo always waits till the last

minute but gets it done alright anyway, like the time I heard when the Theatre Guild asked her to do the uniforms, since she knows all that stuff and can sew. Well, Jean says they were both in Billings the night before the opening, with machine and material in a motel room all night! They never asked her to do them again even though it was the best uniforms they ever had. Jo'll be like "What are you worried about?" when she waltzes in that afternoon, everybody thinking the stuff won't fit. Or the cake for the wedding even, and the suits, which didn't fit the night before! Somehow it all gets taken care of, maybe she'll just Call On You, and you know it is time to Serve With Pride, yeah. We gotta hurry!

This time she probably could have used her talent for postponing things I bet; everybody is biting their nails. Even I get this bitterness at the thought of the loss if the doctors can't do anything. But we don't have enough information and we're anxious, waiting either for jubilation or mourning.

Tonight Rich Davis came over to play Chess, his big news was what Brian and Richard Miller told him about his game. Evidently some shit about how he gets in bad positions during his early mid-game combinations, but he doesn't understand this, all they were doing was patting themselves on the back by taking on the role of commentators when neither of them could survive one minute with a real player. None of us could but if Rich would only study and not pay attention to the rest of us pretenders, he's young and has the snap, he could go somewhere. You can tell when you're playing him, because even though he doesn't seem aware of it, his manner shows him drifting along in about a two-move mode, confident, playing an obvious game with inferiors. Then when you leave it open or give him a poser, he'll just watch it longer, lean forward, and maybe not notice when he hums to himself a little louder; and then, watch it. He has the talent for the flash, but needs to study the book in order to break away from his style and to establish the habits that get him by between flashes.

He was giving me this stuff about learning disability, I don't know why but I think it was because he was shaken, hurt, by the tone Brian & Richard took. I wish I was there to counterbalance it if there were unanimous...he probably lost three games in a row like he'll do on down days, then they quit playing, not like I do, I'll wait until he gets mad and talks to himself: "I better put up a fight..." He never loses after that stage. But the schools fucked him over with Look-Say, and turned him into your apparent-dyslexic with idiot-savant coloring when he could pass for your normal excellent mind with some verbal practice.

Sally has been giving me *Awake!*, the Jehovah's Witness outreach organ, because I have made the error of talking to her. But we play, even if it isn't the same kind of fun we get out of it, like, I'll comment favorably on their resistance to patriotic mumbo-jumbo, and being drafted, leading up to wishing out loud that they were avid tax-protesters and preached against Government and Law unequivocally. "But the Lord is the one who is going to do away with the governments…" etc, etc. Well, I say, hasn't he had his human flunkies do his dirty work before? Shouldn't we consider it our duty to God to actively assist the decomposition of Satan's form of social organization, the State? But she resists, manfully even if I may say so.

Richard gets off on these three-hour debates with her and isn't quite so bashful to say, "Well, the bible isn't written by any but human hands." I've never seen a Christian quite so tolerant and politely persistent before … she's a credit to her church!—which reminds me of the thought I had about Larry, who is Lutheran, that the most insidious aspect of Christianity is that as a by-product of devotion, practitioners tend naturally to develop the requisites of smooth and pleasurable society: unassuming but frank, polite but not obsequious. They listen, too, which is the supreme consideration, and carefully, even if they do exhibit blind spots or immovable prejudices at times.

I tell him that anyway it gives her practice and us the opportunity to observe the articulation of a world-class system, even if it's only one of the three contenders for

Champion. "Ideology, memes, viral structure, steps-to-the-program," I mumble at him, "like in Chess, watching the subsets of contingency schedules kick into operation…"

So now she has lent me some massive tome on Bible interpretation and I was interested since I love all keys and Code-Cracking stuff, especially literary, but with the time problem around here so far I've only gleaned a good name for use in allegory, Abe Eden, which is derived from Abaddon, a powerful symbolic role. I don't have the heart to give her the line about how all conversation is reducible to the trading of one long pair of names, or sometimes advertising brochures for one's social sub-group: "We demand X and the benefits of membership are: …" and so on. We have the literal one and must recruit for the shadow one, or something even discouraging applicants.

Formulas

1. It is said, Now that Linda's rug-rat—name of Jay—is one year old or more, She ought to feed it something more than that soy-protein pap. Some real food, they say.

2. Ever since Elly passed out at work and got fired because the boss knew it was from too much tooting of crank and moved back to Gillette to live with her 18-year-old son's 20-year-old pal; and ever since Sally got suicidally depressed and conceived a crush on a guy she thought she wasn't good enough for, with the result that she grew embarrassed and moved back with her ole man who beat her and took away her car, Linda's two most trustworthy babysitters are no longer there to switch off with.

3. So now Linda switches off with Sally, who's a pariah for being a member of the drug-scandal-tainted women's commune (and married to a dealer yet—the girl we traced as the source of [1] above). Linda chewed out Elly pretty hard for letting Jay dive down the stairs and then spanking him; Elly pals around with Sally and

apocrypha has them in a significant scene discussing Welfare, maltreatment, and Linda.

4. Linda's been sort of staring at everyone she knows ever since she got the call from Welfare which detailed what they planned to do with her now that they'd been tipped off.

5. So how many truckloads of gravel can the company move in three days if Ed was the piano player?

• • •

1. Mention of Sarah before she had been forgotten used to bring on a shaking of heads. Her only close friend was the fellow who worked for Mountain Bell and parked a Harley outside the motel room right on Main Street; he had speed and they both worked hard on the ABATE anti-helmet lobbying effort.

2. Bill says that Sarah's former ole man in Phoenix put the law onto her, which was why we heard she had been crying in the bars she was kicked out of Christmas eve and thereabouts for a week, before she got fired.

3. He overheard her explaining how they came and took away the child.

4. Jack and Dave used to go over to her house with weed and party when they got off work, but they never porked her, of this I am sure. She did not earn the same leers as some others AH HAVE KNOWN.

5. The last we heard she'd been arrested for stripping off

her clothes in a bar in Gillette and dancing nude on the pool table. Shades of somewhere in Massachusetts. She was always planning to go to the doctor about the rash on her arms.

• • •

1. Jimmy hit town again a while back and surprised us all by playing a good game of Chess; we'd never found out since we never asked him. After the games one night we all got drunk and he insisted on calling his girlfriends around Utah and Colorado, collect. I got to talk to May. He said she had six children and gave a pained expression.

2. Jeff is going to Hong Kong this week after failing to make enough money to live on in the National Guard. He's the unofficial Chess champ of the town. This trip will use up his savings, and we're sorry to see him go, but he has to get out of America.

3. Jimmy wanted to give me advice; Jeff told me to count my blessings.

Being Against Motherhood Does Not Go Over in Peoria

It was a dark and stormy night during my quest—in convoluted, tritely self-referential sentence structure—through the Land of Metaphor. "You won't win any awards," said a voice, "for cutesy passages through the Arch of Introduction."

I looked around, and the voice, fading, added, "Besides, the Contest is Over."

"Until next year!" I shouted, shaking my fist. But my voice failed to carry, muffled by the underbrush of Obscure Reference. Frustrated, I resolved to quit right then and there, but the mosquitoes (symbolizing irritation) began to bite, providing me with incentive for a plunge through the brambles and pine branches common in the Forest of Words. Besides, had I not undertaken this quest for my lady-love? I wore her colors, and no knight was I should mere loss of direction cause me to throw up my hands in disgust and go back home to bed.

This time it seemed as if I'd internalized the aforementioned underbrush for good, but this wouldn't stop me either, although it promised to stop many others.

Before long I'd been stopped again, but this time because I had caught a glimpse of light. It faded quickly, proving once more that science is no help in providing materialist expansions—prosaic, as in swamp gas—for will-o'-the-wisps, Faery lights, which I resolved to track down and bring back dead or alive. I tripped over the underbrush, and fell face first into the mud, recalling the time when Sam—or was it Frodo?—did the same thing, well, it was after Boromir got killed, anyway, and there were ghosts and visions under the murk, probably like the old oil & tar pits that dinosaurs are reputed to have fallen into.

There were ghosts here, too, and it smelled, even though I was drowning and shouldn't, by right, have been able to detect this, appropriately decayed. "If you don't get up out of the mud pretty quickly," said one of the spirits, "you're going to be dead."

"Bluh buh bimmah blunnha," I gurgled, trying to say, "Just a little longer." Now the mud was in my lungs for sure, and as I grew dizzy from lack of oxygen my pleasure grew. I saw fantastic visions, dangerous things because they make you want to stay and drown a little longer. But wait…someone had dragged me out! I was staring up at the night sky, symbol of regretted redemption.

An ancient man slapped me. "I am the Old Wise Man in The Story," he said.

"So what else is new?"

"You're making me wince, you jerk, and for that you must pay."

The world is cruel, I decided, as he kicked me in the head so hard that I passed out. "And most lies are ripoffs," he added, "representing a firm grasp of the obvious."

Once I Thought I Knew
By Tribunal O.D.

Once I thought I knew what was the most beautiful sight in the world, and I told someone about it, because we were both walking by and so I could comment without seeming to come out of the blue with a stale image.

There was a girl sweeping the sidewalk in front of us and the sunlight was mid-morning, not too bright or hot, and I anyway was feeling good like you do after a drunk even when I hadn't had one last night and you take vitamins…IT struck me, I was overwhelmed with the sensation of properness. "That's the most beautiful sight in the world," I told this guy.

"What?" he asked, oblivious. I almost got mad at him for being such an insensitive dumb-bell.

"What?! A pretty girl working, that's what!" is what I replied. Then he looked and nodded, but you could see he didn't feel it, he was just humoring me. It didn't strike me that maybe he was higher up on some scale of initiation and had seen one even more beautiful, one that made all the rest look tired and commonplace.

But I wanted to go interrupt her working, it must

have been a surge of mania but I felt like I could do so and not be stared at as if mad, I could go and say, "Let's go!" and she'd go, or whatever, and it would work. Must have been an aftertaste or a residual of the perfect feeling I had, and I didn't heed it because I've heeded those things before and found different. We walked by and left perfection because if we touched it like Heisenberg, we would have ruined it.

Now for a long time I lacked this, and the memory faded like they do. I played some Chess once in a while and got a Thang runnin' like then, like this: when you're on top of it all the way through the game, you're concentrating Hot and not an illusion like the false confidence you get now and then which quickly gets slapped down. No, this time you KNOW what is happening, and for some reason it seems as if the enemy doesn't really have any good moves to make! because even if the move is like, good, yours is better! into a cascade of joy when the other guy is playing automatically and you can anticipate it all, he's not bad because he beats you every other time when you're not at your peak, then the bold stroke, hah! and as a matter of fact some of the people at the Coffee Bar gasped! Ah, yes! Is he mad!? Refreshing.

Yeah, once I thought I knew what was the most beautiful sight in the world, and now I know, and I doubt whether it is okay to reveal the secret, if the gods be watching. I had a chance to see it some other times and didn't, because I was too busy with the Matters At Hand as a manner of speaking, and I know that was a mistake now. You gotta look around a lot to catch them sneaky rascals peeping out of the corner at you just waiting to electrify everything and make your life miserable because they know they'll be hiding mos' the time where you can't find 'em. You can look, and you can give chase, but for some reason they don't want to be used too much.

But the more I think about it all the time now, the less I can hold it back any more. The most beautiful sight in the world is a rosy flush in a triangular area at the top of a woman's chest, no lie. Simple, yet true, I swear. Damn!

That Then I Scorn to Change My State

> I'm forced to do a certain job that ill befits a spy—
> selling loaded guns to girls who say they want to
> die. I get my satisfaction, though I get no thanks;
> they never tell their shame to find the chambers
> full of blanks.
>
> — Farmer Green

I don't normally get so shook up over little things. Some silly mice woke me up a few days ago, playing around with my whiskers. I laid there for a while pretending to be asleep. They were happy, cheerful, probably just had some cheese. I haven't seen any other cats for a long time, so I've been lonely, and I wanted to play with them. I stretched out and then rolled over, which cats never do, to show them I was willing to let bygones be bygones for awhile. They responded by jumping over my stomach one by one, which was cute.

We played for ten minutes or so. I batted them around with my claws drawn in, which they loved. Let one ride on my back. But I got too rough, unintentionally, and hurt one. They felt betrayed and ran off, scampering and squeaking. Come back, delicate ones, you're all I have. I'll try to keep from nipping you. But no. They'll never be back.

Such a truce is doomed from the start. They can never trust me, and I can't trust myself. I think I'll go catch a nice crispy lark for dinner tonight, and swallow it in huge gulps.

> Science isn't value free but surgeons aren't sadists.
> Beauty after all, is in the eyes of the rapist. Bid me
> use a scalpel and with loving cruel precision, I'll file
> another X-ray and refuse to make incisions.
>   — Green, et al, in *Green vs. Jane*

K. Goes to the Lecture

It was during this time, while rumors of the Bank's imminent closing filled the air, that K. met his friend the police-woman while wandering the streets.

"You gave me a fright," K. told her, looking at her bunched-up red hair and wondering whether or not she had an ivory comb.

"Terror can take many forms," she replied. "Why, for instance, it struck us oddly down at the station that you were never terrified during the whole month-and-a-half when I visited you nightly and told you a completely fabricated story of my father's protracted death from cancer. Each night I came down, having spent hours being coached by the Leaders in just how I was to lead the conversation, and we all thought that we had done a bad job of it…we thought you had begun to suspect, that you had found us out, that you knew we were testing you, and why, and what the result would be."

K. pulled at a forelock and smiled. "I never suspected until recently," he said. "But really, does it matter?"

She gestured to her massive German shepherd. "Oh, yes. Let me explain. If you knew that everyone you knew was plotting against you, it would throw an X factor into our calculations. You might conclude that you were going crazy, and seek professional help, at which point you might be drugged or admitted to a hospital, and all our work would have been in vain. Or you might realize the whole truth, and refuse to cooperate, or kill yourself. If you knew that we were trying to drive you crazy in a carefully planned way, you might go crazy in the wrong way. To actually see the extent of our power might have been the straw that broke the camel's back."

K. grew pensive, frustrated at the gabby girl. Couldn't she get to the point? "Look," he told her, "It was obvious to me that you were prostrating yourself, making yourself available to me, and that events had contrived to make you emotionally vulnerable, alone, unhappy, and burdened with bills. You had no man to help you out, and here I was. But the best laid plans…" he drifted off, began mumbling.

His friend the police-woman had to leave and go to police some more places, so K. was left standing, still frustrated. Why couldn't he explain? Just then an acquaintance of K.'s, the revolutionary burgher, hailed him from the other side of the street, in the doorway of a corner beer-hall.

"K.! K.!" he called, interrupting K.'s thoughts. "Come on over, have a beer with me!"

Inside the beer hall were about five impeccably dressed young men with impassive expressions, each of whom turned to gaze as K. entered. "Funny," thought K., "I haven't seen them around here before. Probably just some more intelligence agents on a little R & R."

"Over here," called K.'s friend the revolutionary burgher. "You must hear about the latest development in revolutionary theory!"

The barmaid brought K. a beer, and the revolutionary burgher began to speak.

"Well," he said, "we both know that conditions are intolerable, right?" He paused. "Right?"

"Yes, oh yes," K. said distractedly.

"Good!" cried one of the impeccably dressed young men. "Get him saying 'yes' right off the bat!"

"And we both know that there's no organized way of taking matters into hand, right? Well, then it's clear that the only thing to do is…" and the burgher drifted off, waiting expectantly for K. to fill in the gaps.

K. speculated for a while in silence, and spoke on a few of the various options available, pointing out that most of them were poor.

"But isn't wanton murder and wholesale slaughter and violence the only thing left to us?" the burgher asked, petulantly.

"Oh, you tire me so!" K. exploded. "Of course it isn't. You've made it so obvious that only a fool could disagree! Why don't you just hire your patsies? Is it because of the budget cutbacks?"

Case Studies

John Z. was a very intelligent child who early on learned that a ruling class needs to keep its base in submission by feeding them confusing lies. When he entered analysis at age 30 he was a semi-successful businessman, but his frustration with friends and partners was beginning to put stumbling blocks in the way of further progress toward his goal of total transformation.

Early on in the consultation it became clear that John Z. had great potential for integrating the disparate figures in his preconscious. It was revealed that he had during adolescence learned the value of persuasion, since he had managed to convince his parents to quit their church and instead donate their money to themselves. He reported telling his mother that, "It doesn't make you feel any better, mom, and it costs you money that you might as well use on yourself." Apparently the sheer bulk of people who needed convincing had stunned him into a psychic catatonia, and he lost touch with the early learning that promised strategic goals that admitted of implementation.

"I want a world where there aren't any more Mormons coming to my door and prostrating themselves at the feet of a massive delusion," John Z. told me. "I want the moonies to go to the airport with bombs instead of flowers, I want Khomeini to quit quoting the Koran, I want the headlines to say that the Pope is dead of Toxic Shock Syndrome. I want the churches to fall into disuse and disrepair, and I want people to quit telling me to render unto Caesar."

His co-workers, it seemed, were leaving Bibles in his desk and Norman Vincent Peale quotes under the windshield of his car. Resolution of the conflict was aided in that rigorous anti-authoritarians like John Z. tend to establish transferences.

I prescribed several books and tapes, and held meetings with a number of anarchists, inviting John Z. to attend. Through discussion, John Z. had the observation that those who hate god need him as much as those who profess to love or fear gods. "Really, who cares?" he asked. "The whole ontological dispute doesn't make a bit of difference for our lives." We discovered a model for a project, seeing that active attack usually strengthens the resolve of religious fanatics, and proceeded to flesh out a theory of indirect ridicule. "Much like a bacteria that recuperates from antibodies and turns them to its own use," I pointed out, "virulent attacks on the flower of the rottenness will make it bloom. We must seek to 'poison' the 'agar agar' of fanaticism, as it were, to turn the unconverted masses against the liars."

"Why, yes!" said John Z. "I'll never get anywhere shooting at something that lives on lead; the best thing I can do is withdraw my support, my habit of legitimizing them by providing them with a counter-foil. Then I can pursue their destruction by urging others to do the same!"

When I last heard from John Z. he was still engaged in his project of worldwide revolution, and reasonably satisfied with his progress. My efforts, linked with his, to bring more people toward individuation, offers us a sustaining objective, and daily we see more evidence that conditions are ripe for destruction of the old order.

Bob B. came to my door one day understandably obsessed with the supercession of the organization of production. From youth onward he had correctly perceived the problem of hierarchy and class society and its relationship to the totalitarian nature of modern industrial commodity economies.

"Death on roller skates!" he cried out, "They purchase atom bombs for Christmas presents! They steal your dreams and try to sell them back to you! And every single force apparently lined up in opposition is guilty of rank complicity! They distract us with circuses, and the only thing left when the image fades is a sour taste in our mouths!"

Further investigation revealed that Bob B. was quite well aware of the exigencies of the spectacle, and informed in the particulars of commodity production. "They have to organize scarcity so that we'll continue to buy their vile pretties. Productive forces are sufficient to provide us with the bare necessities and allow us room for play, but they hire a million different breeds of cop to police the empire and prevent us from rising up and seizing our lives, from repossessing our mortgaged souls! We're all billionaires, but they throw us in jail if we want to quit being slaves!"

This case provided special difficulties in that success in any terms depended to some extent on the participation of a number of others; this was further complicated by the realization that any scheme to elicit such participation is imperiled by the tendency for oppositional groupings to assume hierarchical characteristics and to devolve into their presumed enemies; to become, in a word, just another coven of cops.

I reminded him that Fritz Perls let the cat out of the bag when he admitted that individual health was contingent to a great extent on external conditions, and he concurred, offering that Freud's milquetoast call for the transformation of despair into mere garden variety unhappiness was necessary but insufficient. "How will it be," he asked, "with kingdoms and with kings, when whirlwinds of rebellion shake all shores? Do they think that we'll stand for a reduction of our misery? They're going to get wiped out so thoroughly that quantum leaps will seem like slow motion!"

I prescribed frequent doses of beer and told Bob B. that should he continue with his project he would likely start seeing more favorable results soon. The decay of international capital, we agreed, was bringing on a crisis of astounding proportions, and it was only a matter of time before those previously mentioned others would be joining him on his quest.

Doug S. felt stifled and insulted from the day he was born. An artist and aesthete by nature (though certainly no dilettante), he complained that "This culture is dead," and "the pap they feed us wouldn't nourish a beriberi baby." His early works, an attempt to rectify the situation by filling the void, were suppressed and crowded out by the pervasive junk; this later led to his expulsion from an art factory that he had infiltrated. Especially intrigued by the qualities of other cheap and offhand artworks that had been similarly persecuted, he set about weaving the disparate threads into a comprehensive whole, proposing to revolutionize the art world by exposing the Conspiracy.

He and several like-minded fellows had spent some time prior to the consultation involved in this project, and were seeing some measure of success. But Doug S. was stymied. "We aren't having the impact we thought we'd have," he complained. "Everywhere our attempt to pull the covers off the lie have been taken as more false works. They pretend that my project is yet another cutesy color-coordinated Miro painting to mesh with the decor in your living room."

His project, a church/ideology faith whose tenets simply cannot be transcribed here, struck a chord with me, and appeared to be effective within the limits placed on such works by the reigning powers. But the violent critique of everyday life that it offered internally was being passed off by stylish adherents who used it to gain laughs at cocktail parties, and worse, few of them were sending money. Doug S. was literally starving with his wife and children, trying to supersede modern culture while trapped inside it.

I contributed my efforts as best I could to his project and encouraged him to continue, with more ferocious and unrecuperable ("hard-core") being played up if possible. In other words, for a parody to be successful, it must be rigorous, I pointed out. A religion must promote its money lust to the utmost; a work of art must not fail to be the cheapest looking, sloppiest piece of unthought-out junk possible. And all skill must be marshaled to invent more and more specious and spurious bullshit to support such art in terms of theory.

At last contact, Doug S. was continuing bravely, and is expected to. To some extent he has not resolved the conflict between participating in art and attempting to expose it; however, in time we are likely to see that his effort has weakened the stranglehold that the art empire holds on us.

—DokTor Gerry ETC, HPU

Number 8, Number 8

Smoky used to live at the Edwards, right next to Kay, the 90-year-old guy from Japan who used to be a bouncer at the Hotel Rex when it was a cat-house at the turn of the century. Kay gets this Japanese newspaper about twice a week, and he never had a wife, but Smoky drank and didn't have either.

I used to see him when I'd pass down the hall, since being the Authority in the absence of the owners meant he collected the rent for them and swept the stairs. So he was a busybody and always knew what was going on; he'd be the one to tell you to turn the music down, this crotchety old man so drunk you didn't want to fuck with him or make him mad. About half the time his door was open and one or another of the street Indians would be in there, and you could see this paleolithic face staring at the TV with Smoky, and a big old bottle on the table along with some beers for chaser. Smoky always had about forty bottles of pills right on the same table and I always wished he was corrupt enough to want to sell some of the good ones for booze money but you never got anywhere with these guys, these World

War Two vets with their world war two ideas about morality: if the doctor gives you something to get wasted on, why, go ahead, but if it's some punk-age kid, well, bullshit on that. Fuck.

Ed Gardner I asked about it, since I knew he had cancer, and he was some kind of crazy to boot, once got in hot water for rape or something, and used to bust up his little rooms on a regular schedule of hopeless rage until they got him hooked on every downer in the book and his teeth fell out. He used to hang around late, late at night because there isn't (wasn't) a single other person in this whole god-damned town that would talk to him for more than ten seconds… the waitresses being about it: "What'll you have today, Ed."

But he never came through even with all the artful devices…he didn't need the money, and it must have been some catholic upbringing in him (he told me the whole Mass in Latin one night, drool and all, in a transport of piety) that prevented this transfer of doctor-authority.

So Smoky was, beside Kay and Ben, the oldest guy there, who had been there the longest, and probably couldn't have told you shit about all the different things and people he'd seen and known throughout his reign as the shadow-government of the Edwards. More like some rhythmical consciousness that comes to all these drunks: hospital is where it starts, when you wake up maybe, and then it goes in steps: money (somehow), familiar faces and street corners, red & blue lights, or vomit all over your face, and shirt, then bars on the door and back to the dry-out center. They get into the sacred when they break the stride, either when no money comes through and they see the faces only without being drunk—everybody is different!—or at the dry-out sessions, and both of 'em are hell-sacred, torture places. Smoky must have, since he didn't go on binges... this slow, steady decline, like a scientist measuring it out to avoid the bumps...had a different rhythm; measured out by the people around him. Every year the owners went on vacation for awhile; every day Ben Jordan would be up early and in a foul mood unless he took his medication, in which case he'd be telling you baseball scores from 1920; every week some new drifter got a room with his last ten bucks and then vanished. In slower time, there would be all the reformed drunks who were trying to be Biblical scholars, like the one who had a Ph.D. on prehistorical middle east stuff, or these failed psychologists like Bob who gets fired from dishwashing jobs; maybe some deaf old jerk who was a cook until he got his pension from the government and just doesn't care about anything except expressing his contempt for everybody. These guys would stay a few months, maybe a year, and become part of the family, the anti-family of all black sheep.

So anyway, this guy Doug Smith that I know drifted through town and I told him the Edwards was the chapel door, if you wanted to be entered into the lowdown section you had to pass through a residence there. If you wanted to really earn your name you had to be kicked out, but since he took off before he had a chance to do this, he left a dead black cat in his freezer for the owners to discover.

Doug was in number eight, where Smoky used to have quiet parties. One day nobody saw him for awhile and they went up and knocked on the door but all they found inside was Smoky dead. Ben says his skin was all black. When Doug was there you never would have known some old worthless shit had pissed in the same bed, and then died there when some spirit came out of the same closet to cart off all the people fool enough to rent that room at that place, the last stop before hell or Sheridan if you're gonna stay alive for a while. Nobody cared except the owners who had to clean up all the shit from twenty years of not sweeping under the bed, and Ben, who's getting old, and maybe somebody who had to update his file at Social Security. Sorta weird, like the exact opposite of some king whose ministers would hide the body until they found somebody they could elevate immediately after the announcement, and railroad it through the Senate.

Sensations

I'm forgetting the first sensation, which irritates me and causes me to feel despair, I'm juggling, I'm trying to visualize something with my eyes open, I'm building sand castles, but no, I'm trying to build real castles, two in the same place with different designs (I'm splitting into two, no, three people), I'm jumping back and forth between two transformer plates like in the science fiction novels, I'm turning colors like a chameleon, I'm trying to synthesize, I'm a phenomenologist, holding up more than one idea in my consciousness, superimposing disparate images, trying to do it just right so that I can perceive an ordered whole that will stay together rather than flying apart and disintegrating, I'm building a geodesic dome of twigs with my hands tied behind my back, I'm putting together a model ship in a glass bottle, I'm locking into a microtelescope that keeps getting blurry, I'm scratching my face and wishing I had even a few tablets of codeine. I'm on the biggest N-dimensional Rubik's cube, called the mind, I'm trying to cement a shattered mirror back together again, trying to fit the pieces into something that works (Grace! Elegance!), shaving an edge here for this contingency, tagging that percept or concept, this context or that question with tracers and chains of reasoning memorized for future further study and resolution, it's ping pong, this one leads unexpectedly back to that strut, that beam, which isn't strong enough to hold it, I have to go and tear out the whole corner and build it again, but I have to hurry over to the other side because the roof is sagging, it needs propping up immediately, the thing is a house of cards, it's tumbling down, no, wait, it's going to be okay, I have to put a drop of Krazy Glue® at each joint, it's a fusion machine, I need more laser heat, the magnets aren't strong enough, it's going out of control, shut it down now! before the whole outbuilding melts! and build the magnets over again, check the timing programs, rewrite the program on the computer to get the bugs out so they can coordinate the magnet pulses, rebuild the batteries, they got all fucked up from the overload, I don't even have time to worry about...

Here's the man with the gun, he wants me to work faster, why doesn't he realize that I'm going as fast as I can, no, he says it's okay for now, just make sure I meet the next hundred and fifty deadlines on time, the stress is incredible, I feel like shit, this is all coming to nothing, the project is broken, I wish someone would murder me, I only enjoy things when they leave me alone, I work better then, it pleases me when my art is proceeding, how do they expect me to work under this stress! and they keep taking everything away, they won't let me keep anything I finish, they feed me dog food, I never see anyone, all I have to keep me company at night is my nightmares. Oh, the beauty! One moment to relax and I see it, I get a glimpse, who CARES about the guns, they can't hurt me when I have the vision! I can see the finished project, and a million more stunning sights, come up before my eyes! If I had this tool I could get it done in a minute, I have to wait, and work at it, I have to build the tool, I don't know how.

It gives me peace to figure out how to build the tool, but my peace is gone when I see how much is left for me to do, in every minute the structure decays, mutates, changes, needs different tools.

I want more time. If I can't have water (I set my teeth, grim, determined), then...I'll build a mirage.

Conflicting Virtues

For Elayne; may she grow rich.

"Truth is what you profess in order to avoid being shot by the Committees."

I was working behind a desk in the front office of the Citizens' Committee to Abolish Drug Abusers main building one day when Jake "Fat Man" Alderman walked in looking like he owned the place. Only later did I find out that he did. I was just an old teenager at the time, Christian for a Strong America, all that shit. This was just a summer's volunteer stint inspired in part through the agency of public crocodile tears being shed by an upper class first lady who felt that her husband's P.R. called for a little charitable destruction. We were administrative assistants and gofers, helping out in the A building with the distillers, offloading the Zyklon-B, firing up the ovens, herding the latest batches from the inner city two thousand miles away and six hundred miles in diameter. The liberals long ago having been either toasted or taught otherwise to keep their mouths shut, there really wasn't anyone left to protest; but at the time I never suspected that the camps should be protested. I had helped out with the enforcement of the early gun control measures which greatly facilitated the liberals' oxygenation, see, all you had to do was take arms away from the liberals' enemies and then they could be rounded up. But the Fat Man's presence was my first inkling that something was wrong.

"Can I help you?" I asked, fingering the cross around my neck.

"You are, son," he said patronizingly, "You are."

That set me off; I had seen his pictures in the papers. There seemed to be pretty strong evidence that linked him to the mysterious drug manufacturing centers, wherever they were. Of course he was also well connected with people in the House and Senate, and had been a good friend of the President's prior to the election, I think. After all, it sometimes seems that the newspapers report different things…

Not long afterward I was assigned to the distilleries for a while. We weren't the least bit wasteful at these installations, no sir. There was plenty of good material to be extracted from the bodies before they were burned, even though they were drug addicts.

While there I fell into conversation with one fellow, an oddball who I had just lately resolved to report to the Citizen's Committee for Normalcy should he continue to behave in deviant fashion. This, it turns out, was the fateful hour of my life, for it was there and then that I first found out what the extracts were and to what use they were put.

"Try some of this," the oddball told me, holding out a syringe.

"What do you mean? What is it, a drug?"

"No, no," the fellow told me, "it's only one of the vitamin-mineral extracts. It'll pep you up."

I'm not sorry now, though I suppose that were I the same person as before I would be. I took the injection and was instantly treated to a body sensation not unlike orgasm which lasted for about ten hours.

"What is it again?" I asked.

"Sucker!" the guy shouted. "It's drugs! It is *the* drug, the one we keep hauling them for, the beta endorphins we squeeze out of their brains!"

I left the place then and made my way to the inner city, overcome with shame and curiosity. It was easy to find people who sold the drug, as a matter of fact they sought one out quite actively, considering that their markup was nothing to sneer at. They will go to any length to get one to try the drug just once, I know because I started dealing. I used to wonder where the money went until I met the Fat Man again on the other side of the fence. He gives a proportion to the anti-drug lobbyists so that they can propagandize in favor of harsher and ever harsher deterrence measures, and he pays off the Citizens' Committee to Halt Drug Importation so that they will bust the lone entrepreneurs. This of course raises his income since the product has fixed manufacturing costs and a steady demand. Finally he probably has to pay the overhead on the incinerators so that the taxpayers don't squawk. I'll probably see the inside pretty soon, entering from the wrong door so to speak. We all have to pay for our pleasure.

I'm glad the liberals never had the guts to legalize drugs when they were in power way back when because then it never would have been profitable enough for the Fat Man to invest his money in the production and distribution networks. I swear it on a stack of needles.

Kidnapped!

1. Once I was a key player on "Bob"'s all-star team. I was Gerry Reith, High Pope of the Unpredictable. I had worked hard to get where I was.

2. Then I blundered. I committed the Impossible Sin, which can't be described, since it doesn't exist.

3. "Bob" grew enraged at my error, and withdrew his protective cloak of emanations.

4. I retained my great spiritual powers of course, but I was naked to the Detektor devices of the Conspiracy.

5. They located me in short order as I spun out plunging ever deeper into the confusion of one who has strayed from the path.

6. I was kidnapped, and brutally murdered.

7. My body was shipped to the secret base on the moon for preparation as a burnt offering to the Unnameable One.

8. But back at home, my protege, Tribunal Overdrive, was busy.

9. He got in contact with the elusive Doktor Moore, an ally of "Bob"'s, and convinced him to mount an effort to save me.

10. Doktor Moore and his heroic crew blasted off!

11. They raided the Con's HQ and made off with my crumbling remains.

12. At Doktor Moore's advanced laboratory they worked day and night.

13. Finally I was sustained on the Supersecret Death Support System.

14. They proceeded to reconstruct my memory from the ground up.

15. Recently I was boosted back to life by a secret process that was discovered by "Bob" back in fifty-eight, but which was suppressed by the Con's agents in the patent offices.

16. So here I am again, but I'm not the same any more.

Issues in Suspension

"We're all necessarily separate from each other," the teacher said. Class was just beginning. Outside: Wilson was coming closer, still distinctly late, the unknown, on the way to existence, presence. I saw him through a window of vulnerability past the trash barrel that blocks the view of those critics on the other side of the room.

Lately, I thought, Wilson had gone off the deep end, into cheap religion, spurious answers to irrelevant questions. Ghosts, mediumship, all that stuff that he had earlier pointed out as trivial.

"I'm talking to you," the teacher said to me.

"Fuck you," I muttered, "I'm busy, I have to work this out first."

I got lost in the hours somehow, something that the Law prohibits. Later when I woke up again, remembering to remember myself in pursuit of a sterile Ouspenskian exercise, adjusted to suit my own ends, my art, the class was different, some science mumbo-jumbo from the mouths of babes, undergrad filling in for prof.

"Paradigm shift," I heard him say before I fell asleep,

the drugs working. "Neutron planet, so dense as to be incomprehensible. Models, cheap plastic imitations."

"Yeah, right," said someone next to me. "She has the biggest pair in the room by a long shot."

"Decay," the voice told me. "It's not worth the effort given the contrasts in the environment between tension and release."

Finis . . .

Variations on a Theme

Not long ago I dreamed I was at home, downstairs in the I living room reading a book. Suddenly I am startled by the smell of smoke and I look around, spying flames licking up through the cracks in the floorboards. The cellar is on fire!

I rush to the cellar door and open it, getting blasted by the flames that pour out. Stepping onto the stairs that lead down, I fall through into the inferno. Scrambling to get up I run through the fire and find an extinguisher. After combat that seems more futile the longer It continues, I manage to put out the flames.

I try to discover the source of the fire, but to no avail. I poke around for hours, dreading to think that it could have been spontaneous combustion; for this would mean that the fires could break out again at any moment, consuming the entire house. Sadness strikes me when I imagine the loss of the old and valuable books in the attic.

Another time I dream of living through several scenes in my daily life and getting exhausted. I realize that I am in danger of dying from depletion of *elan*. But a strange thing occurs, and like a one-celled animal I watch dispassionately while my body splits in two. The other body lapses into a coma, and I catch it as it drops to the floor and stow it away in the closet. I am dismayed to think that my time is still limited, that the split has just staved off same kind of reckoning, and that I must find something to recharge us both and catalyze reunification. What's worse is that it is clearly impossible to get enough extra life for the recombination. The clone body lies forgotten but once in a while I check on it. I am filled with fear at the thought that if I ever do manage to revive it It will become angry with me for my neglect.

Recently I dreamed of looking into a mirror. "Funny," I think, "I can't see anything." I flip on the light switch, and it horrifies me to find that I've been murdered. My face is bruised and the back of my head is gone. Only shreds of flesh and dried blood are left. I turn off the lights again, feeling ill at the sight of my blasted brains, and wonder how I am ever going to reassemble the drying flecks of matter that must be on the floor. "This is going to get in the way of my normal relations," I recall saying to myself. "One can't just wander around looking killed."

In a fourth dream I happen upon a man drowning in a river, and rush in without thinking to save him. After immense efforts I drag him to the river bank, where he falls to his knees and thanks me profusely. Before

I know what I'm doing I slap him on the face and say, irritably, "If you thank me for saving your life you are far from enlightenment."

John told us around the coffee bar several nights ago about what Ardrey thought. He figured decay was inevitable but I objected that observers can always conclude that civilization is falling apart.

"If everything beside the status quo is judged barbaric," said Bob, concurring, "then of course it looks like a descent."

Still, said John, Ardrey's model is a good one. Take the example of the rat population where they all live in a huge cage, and there are tunnels leading out to smaller cages on a periphery. "Dominant males will station themselves and their mates at the end of each tunnel," John told us. "From time to time males from the center colony come out, but they leave, or if they stay they don't even try to mate with the females there…"

"Traveling salesman," Bob interrupted, laughing.

"And then at regular intervals the children leave and go to the center places… "

"Life in the big city!" I yelled, scoring a point.

"Right, yeah. There's all sorts of aberrancy in the center, where the population density is high."

He pauses to eat some of his hamburger. "And then when it reaches a certain point it seems that everyone gets a cue to go berserk, and there is mass violence. Inexplicable because there really isn't any revolutionary lucidity about it, there aren't any organizations, correct lines, it's just time to kill and be killed."

"Chaos," Alan popped in. "The return to formless chaos."

"The individual is negated by the invisible-but-rigid social structure," I offered.

"What happens on the outskirts then?" Bill asked.

"Well," said John with a smile, "they barricade themselves, buy lots of guns, and form survivalist groups, showing no mercy on the ones that wander out their way."

"All dressed up and nowhere to go," said Bob, laughing. We all sat and stared at our plates for a while.

When Matthew and his parents arrived, talk turned to the tone of his Strad, and plans for the Berg concerto he was planning to perform. We listened to his report on the latest chapter of Spengler, which he was reading during his leisure hours, and I promised to bring him a tape by the Ramones.

In another dream I am behind the control panel of an enormous, powerful machine. I sweat with dread, knowing that I am charged with important tasks. But I do not know exactly what I must do. On the screen in front of me I monitor various scenes, and by playing with the dials and switches I can call up any images I choose, real or fantasy. I discover that certain controls have an effect on the scene I watch, and I feel like a movie director. This fills me with terror.

It is then that I find that one of the dials can bring me schematics and diagrams; another formulas and functional derivation tables. I spend time with geometric patterns and graphs in motion, with spheres and N-dimensional constructs. This terrain is safer because it is clearer, but more dangerous because the finest error has broad effects. I begin to feel pain as if being tortured. When I blur the images the pain recedes and I can continue to work, but if the images get too vague I lose all control over them and they take on a life of their own, incomprehensible to me. I let go of the control panels for a while and look around; I'm locked in a cage. When I turn back to the screen it is flashing "CORONARY" in red, and I wake up.

Closing Redux

Jo (the name befits her role as generic lover for all sorts of desperate and intelligent young men in Sheridan) pestered me drunk again two nights ago while I was at work crunching numbers. She has a habit of binges, doesn't seem particularly interested in any of the disposable cocks she takes home, and will on occasion when un-partnered totter out the bar and fall into my arms attempting, I suppose, to elicit some response from someone.

Tonight she told me of her conviction that Dale (the horsetrading wheeler-dealer from Texas who owns the place where I work and is Pa to Brent & Brian) is masterminding a plot to destroy the Sheridan Center, close it down, make it go kaput.

"Why is Dale trying to wreck this place?" she wondered for me.

"What?"

"It's obvious, he's doing everything he can to ruin it!"

"Like what?"

"Oh, come on! You don't go serving the Big Horn Executive Club with a dirty banquet room; you don't serve Rotary the same meals two months in a row!"

"What are you talking about, that's just simple mismanagement! It is all LaVerne's fault, it is…just because he doesn't keep hotshot middle management on their toes…"

This, of course, was more proof. "Ha!" she cries. "More proof! You know why he keeps LaVerne here, don't you?"

"What now?" I say. "Isn't this getting a bit melodramatic?"

"It's because Dale used to sleep with her."

"And this is enough to protect a job?"

For Jo it is clear as a bell. "She could break up Dale and Billie." An afterthought, though—"But Billie probably knows about it anyway."

Right, thinks I. They're all over sixty if they're a day. I don't see what it will matter. Or why any of this matters, for that matter. I begin to understand after a while.

"Look," I expound, "You're not being rigorous, scientific about this. You're using the assertion, the hypothesis, as proof of itself, which is invalid."

Bring drunk, Jo nods sagely, missing it all, probably watching the hair on my head or something. "The board forced him to take a leave on the place this summer," she tells me. "They got all pissed off and shafted him."

This is getting tiresome, I thought. "So what? So what? I don't care!"

"But why is he trying to kill the place?"

"Oh, so he can take a tax write-off or something. It's all the coke money, this place is really just a laundromat for the Mafia or something. They're getting rich from Mason smuggling, they need a money sink."

"Be serious," she tells me.

"Yeah, right, be serious. You haven't given me any conclusive evidence to back up these assertions that get you so emotionally worked up. If you're going to be scientific, you take the data, generalize a rule, and then test to see if the rule holds true in cases previously unexplored. So what do you have for me? He keeps on some washed-out help, sure. He lets them insult the good customers, lets them serve bad food, lets them turn the place into a pigsty. This isn't at all enough to go on for generalizing the rule unless you're paranoid."

I pause for breath.

"And more—if it were true, we'd have to find out more evidence of it. If he really wants to do this, wouldn't he be going at it with more vigor? Why does he do some things that are good for the place?"

"It would be too obvious."

"Argument from silence. If that's what he's doing it becomes obvious after a time anyway. He might as well go whole hog."

"But you don't wipe the banquet slate clean, you don't let them all go, you don't give in!"

"More! It has to obey Occam's razor! If there is a simpler answer, that's the one! All your evidence adds up to nothing more than a tired old man who's given up the ghost, who leaves everything in the hands of his corrupt and decadent lackeys! What about the union, he would have let that slide through if he really wanted to bust the place, but he fought it!"

"Dale is smart," Jo warns me, "he's no dummy. You mean to tell me it's just a case of incompetence, the way he has four people working maintenance and the walls haven't been washed in ten years? The grime is so thick you can wipe it off with your fingers in the kitchen alone."

I give a little. "And the walls of the hallways, the brick, I know, I've spent some time trying to do them with a spray bottle and towels, but I just don't have the tools."

"See! See! He's trying to ruin the place!"

"No, he's not. It's just another case of power being blind. If stupidity is an answer, or laziness, then that suffices. He means to do X, but the law of unintended consequences means that Y will result. Among other things, he maybe just doesn't pay attention to details that the lowly ones like us see all the time."

"But why does he keep on all these idiots, these fucking jerks!?"

"I don't know, I don't know. Why worry about it, anyway?"

"It's your job, it's my job, aren't you worried about that?" Now I begin to understand where Jo hails from.

"What can you do about it?" I ask. "You buys your

ticket and you takes your ride. Do your best to prepare for unpleasant events."

"But he shouldn't be allowed!"

"You're making a claim to some sort of authority over him, making a claim to title that isn't just. From where do you derive title?"

Drunks don't see it that way. We haggled for a while, until we got on the subject of drugs, and I elicited a promise.

"What do you need?" she asks, power over me now.

"Need, no, need?"

"Well, what do you want?"

"I like chemicals, synthetic opiates, maybe some Darvon, Percodan."

"How many? I'll get you twelve, I have hundreds, every doctor in town hands me prescriptions."

I'm amazed. "What, your back?"

"Sure! I'm a trained actress, I can get whatever I want!"

Later it ran back onto the unfounded suspicions.

"I tell you, he means to close this place down."

It dawns on me then. We're not just talking about Dale or the Center. I recall, Lord, I recall, who ended up buying all that cheap rock bottom price land in the years after '29, and I recall, I'm now singing the blues, and she says, "He makes money whether this place is open or closed."

He makes money whether this place is open or closed. Tim has a new baby son. I am flat broke. Jo wants to save and go back to school. The rest? They have their ends, and one means, but He makes money whether this place is open or closed. I still don't think he wants to close it down, though. Not Dale, anyway. David? Ronald? Edwin Meese? Come down to the Chase when you need a loan.

An Objective Lesson
By Rev. Tribunal Overdrive

It's often said among the Church elite that the most merciful thing that could happen to the Normals would result if we allowed them to starve. Even non-Church pundits have asserted strikingly similar doctrines, to the effect that to kill these cripples would be doing them a favor. Well, I had an experience the other day that drove home this point.

It began while I was at work, reading the newly issued "Book," by "Bob." I felt a nagging sort of uneasiness that lasted quite a while. I noticed, and noted, a number of specific sensations; among them, a mental analogue of the irritating feeling one gets during a bout of the flu, when, late at night and lying on one side, one breathes through only one nostril since the other is all plugged up. Another was the definite sensation that one eye was asleep, or something, as if everything was one-dimensional, as if one of my two main personalities had just gone into a coma or something.

That was it! I felt undimensional, flat, and vague. "There's only one person here!" I thought, and it hit me like a slap of cold water. I decided that I must be unconscious, and that this is what it must be like to be a normal person; sort of tired and bored with everything. I noticed that there was no "internal monologue" at all, and since I usually have three going on at once, I wondered what had happened.

A wave of panic swept over me as I did my exercises to try to "wake up" again, to re-activate the feedback loop, to come back to consciousness. Nothing helped and the night wore on while I cataloged more and more disturbing symptoms of Normalcy in myself.

Among them, I noticed a general tone, a mode, that swept in and out subtly, like a subtext from *The Twilight Zone*: the feeling that I was on automatic pilot, that if I didn't think about it I'd know what to do next. Immediately I began thinking about what I should do next, and as if by magic, I lost all sense of priority. I felt lost, absurd, naked. Every possible act was equally valuable, and hence equally valueless. It was terrifying. I decided quickly not to reflect on metaphysical matters, hoping not to imprint my new program with any of the implied steps that this state of unconsciousness would articulate for me, but in a flash the whole cascading mess of possible boredoms flooded my thoughts, and I cared not one whit for any of the formerly glistening dialectics and contradictions that only yesterday had fascinated me.

Truly something was wrong. I thought for a moment,

trying to figure out where the sleep had begun. I had been listening to the Talking Heads when I jerked off earlier that evening, looking at drawings in *Heavy Metal* magazine. Perhaps, I wondered, perhaps subliminals are more effective in times like those?

Then it struck me that if this was true, I'd have to find a dealer sometime soon and take a large dose of LSD to wash out all the programs and start over again. What a bother! I'd also have to swear off Eno and his ilk, which would be tiresome.

But wait! Drugs! I remembered that I had taken some downs just a few hours ago! No wonder I couldn't remember my name! I started laughing at the simplicity of it, and one of my co-workers gave me an odd look.

"Probably unconscious," I thought. "The best thing for those types of people would be some good ole eternal sleep."

Anyway, it relieved me to think that after a good night's rest, I'd be back to super-normal. The plunge into dull consciousness had been a sharp reminder of the abyss between myself and other people, and proved to me that for most people, life isn't worth living. Odd, how a drug intended to induce calm had caused me such fear and doubt; stranger still how calm I get when I take too much speed. Ah, well. Vote for me; there's work to be done.

The Pleasure Palace: A Visit
For M.H. & M.V.

It was a late hour on a rainy evening when This Reporter received his assignment to cover the Pleasure Palace. Rain pattered on the ceiling and whipped across the windows of my room in the small downtown hotel; but having worked for fanzines before, I knew the conditions: file before the deadline and expect the usual rates, i.e. nothing. The payoff was in seeing that name in print—and not at one's own expense. Publish or perish; one more credit for the resume sir, one more open door. The rain then was no longer a noise to be enjoyed but an expense to chalk up with the rest to the cost of fame. Off then. Perhaps the trip would be worth it.

•

A bit of history might be in order when covering such hallowed institutions; special conditions, however, render such matters both difficult and unnecessary. For one, tradition has it that Pleasure Palaces have always existed and always will; that indeed they are if anything an inescapable part of the national landscape. Most people are familiar through rumor if not direct experience with the workings of the archetypal Palace. To further bury the dead past it seems that neither accurate nor systematic records are or ever have been kept. One is stuck then with an irritating wham-bam-just-the-facts-ma'am presentation. Theory, set and setting have little role to play. But said it has been that one best gets to the heart of the affair, the power and the glory as it were, through rigorous description.

The Palace in question is an encampment of old red brick buildings in the eternal capital style: evidently some thought is given to the aesthetic sensibilities of those frequent visitors from the realm of professional politics. Therein lies a clue, though of what import I know not: for those tastes whose satisfaction requires no small investment may be said to earn their panderings. The layout of the buildings will seem at first to be random and even aimless, making travel between for the neophyte a bit confusing. A tidbit gleaned from the staff, apocrypha, has it that this apparently thoughtless arrangement was in fact the result of careful planning by a crew whose work was shamefully rendered nil by the late discovery that most would do their inter-building travel by foot rather than by car. Never mind. One gets by.

We have the outside, or at least all of it that is necessary. No need to note the carefully tended patches of brown, the absent wheelchair ramps, let alone the utter disregard for water and sewage draining. Enough medicine on hand, it seems, to nip those frequent outbreaks in the bud. What matters for us are the nuts and bolts, the internal machinery, beauty being skin deep and all that. Fashion is at best a whim, at worst a manipulation. And so for the indoors.

Multitudinous arrays! Racks, spikes, irons! Tools to delight the jaded cognoscenti! Echoing screams! Halls where it is safely assured that the sound of dull sense being rudely awakened has not ceased for centuries! All around the spoor of extraction and the sign of tastefully mopped up wine-like substances. An endless party for those so fortunate as to enter. Never ending games to fill those wasted hours with the joy of regularity and security. Never has the Palace been attacked during wars: never invaded and the walls never breached. Some rumor to the contrary of course floats around, but that? Simply part of the menu. No work need be done by those happy vacationers. All is provided free of charge to the carefree residents and clientele. A cheerless staff avoids appointments with appropriate glee. Schedules in dazzling volume are produced and pronounced void through action: strict observance within the standard infinite variance. It is for the satisfaction of the clientèle's needs that these pointless exercises are made: some must be convinced of a destination in order to fully experience the joy of ne'er arriving, including, of course, those members of the staff that only believe themselves to be!

The activities are for understatement delicious as are all such forbidden fruits for the uninitiated. Every imaginable brand of loving torture can be found to satisfy any possible desire. And yet curious anomalies are found upon interviewing the participants.

"How does it feel?" one might ask of some orgasmic wreck enduring the Nth involuntary application of some finely crafted thumbscrew or other.

"Feel?" comes the reply, "What does that word mean?" Or better yet, they understand: "Feel? I don't feel anything." How cross purposes it seems at first!

At first, yes. For there are as many and as varied responses as there are stimuli...although this is denied by the higher placed and more scientifically minded members of the staff. Take the revealing squeal of one who has just enjoyed the rare treat of having had each and every fingernail removed at once and in a trice while a single chosen tooth was instantly mashed into powder by oh-so-special miniature hydraulic presses. The sought-for terror it seems according to this one's testimony, lies not in the act itself, oh no but in the foreknown inevitability. Why go they willingly to each and every room where such luxurious lacerations are applied?? To staunch the flow of fear! By walking unaided they know that they won't be thrown out to face the unknown! Indeed, one must assume that the woman who chose to have her clitoris first hot-iron seared and then with wrench ripped out would be best off following this path should the terrors elsewhere be so great as to outweigh these.

Horrors worse than they know exist, it seems. How to produce a garden variety horror that will be in contrast a pleasure?

But a further discovery is made. Some of our connoisseurs, it seems, place stock in tales of tables reversed. At random, and consistent with the law of caprice which governs those who govern others, one struggling adoration filled bootlicker or another will be chosen to join the staff. Sometimes, staff members are with relish and entirety against their will violently thrown down among the ranks of the vacationers. Pleasure can be found both in submitting and in watching others submit.

And so we see but a rough overview of the many pleasures available at the Palace. For some the love of pain and the pain of love are enough. For others, regularity alone will suffice, and pains are not registered as such. Others quest after what would be for some intolerable boredom and banality. Still more enjoy most highly the knowledge that Daddy is there, and that though He may at times be somewhat less loving than He might, at least His divine love shows through in that He protects us from Himself when it takes His fancy. In the end we have those lucky few who get their kicks wishing they could do unto others what they bid others to do unto them.

Sad it is that those on the outside, whose numbers are,

admittedly, growing thin, never get to know His mercy. Left to the bitter winds of foul chance and evil struggle, endlessly busy cleaning the rice bowl when the meal is finished and so on, they know not what they miss.

But for those on the inside, consolation can be had. Once in a while they grow insufferably bored (those capable of it), and manage to send out recruiting teams to round up a few whose fresh straining will keep them occupied throughout the lonely and uneventful eras, the winter nights of the state.

> Yr. Faithful correspondent from the other side of the looking glass,
> HPU Gerry Reith

Third Worldview:

And in the third day of my quest I came to an old shop that was the storefront office of a cheap astrologer. He and his wife had evidently been hassled by the police for their shady dealings in the past; upon knocking I detected furtive motions by the curtains in the front window.

"Come in," said the grizzled sage. "We will look in my crystal ball and I will tell you what it is you came to hear."

I wondered what carny this old badger had learned his lines in. We walked past a kitchen that steamed cabbage and cheap potatoes and into a dingy, ill-lit parlor whose walls were evidently not meant to hold the hastily tacked up posters and charts. They had not been in town for long.

"I want to know of the world," I told the man.

"I know you do. You already told me," he said. "The fee for this session will be ten dollars, payable in advance."

I gave him the money and sat at a gesture in the direction of a rickety card table.

"In order to know of the world you must first know of yourself," he intoned. "Look into the crystal ball."

I looked at the ball…it seemed to me to be a bowling ball painted with day-glo by some student of psycho-chic. He began some narrative that I cannot recall, a guided fantasy type muttering that took all responsibility for suggesting images. Then he asked me to tell him what I saw, and I remembered that my eyes were open.

I saw nothing, like when you do an exercise for discovering your blind spot. This was a bit frustrating because I thought I had gone blind.

I told him this, and he said good. "Most people only see the colors and I have to make up a bunch of stuff for them. Just keep at it." Then he gave a laugh.

I continued to keep the blind spot in my gaze, and I saw all sorts of amazing events. Little beach balls of green shouted obscenities at the moon. Elephants cavorted among pine trees. I saw a young woman play eighteen holes of golf in one stroke, the ball bouncing out of each pocket and flying down the fairway to a series of holes in one. Then I saw a herd of poets drinking coffee in a thousand little cafes. And I saw myself engaging in a million different activities, some that I would have done if I had a chance and others that I would not. I was filled with emotion.

"What do you see?" the geezer asked.

"I guess it's me," I told him, "all wrapped up in a mixture of symbol and literal representation."

"Wise young one," he said. "Don't worry about it. Actually it's not you. Most people think that they see themselves whenever they get past the blind spot, but they don't realize that whenever they cut off all outside data they just start making it up to entertain themselves, like a cat playing with a ball of yarn. Most of it is lies."

I had just finished taking a visionary inventory of a huge vault of gems when he said this, and I shook myself up out of it and back to the room.

"Now it is time to look at a portion of the world itself."

I looked back at the globe, the mirror, the round diamond. I was stricken with awe at the first sight. Forests of trees were being mowed down and fed through monstrous machines that spit out flat, ink-covered versions of some sort of wafer. People lined up to buy these wafers and stood motionless while staring at them. Hours later they would vomit up little bits of typeface, obviously in pain. A voice came from all around, saying, This is how men come to know their worlds. It is efficient to filter all the most shocking portions of the world and squeeze them into little bits to be fed out at random. In this way opinion is formed.

Then the scene transformed itself and I stood over a small island. On it slaves toiled under a hot sun for soldiers with machine guns. In the capitol, men came and went, handing out little receipts that the others would use to cash in for more guns. The men who handed out the receipts had one condition: that they be allowed to take whatever the slaves produced. In turn, the men who had the guns would be allowed to live in prosperity when it wasn't their turn on guard duty. Another voice came and said, This is the miracle of the free market. This is what they call capitalism. This is the chief fuel for the fires of the left.

I was immediately shown another scene, exactly like the last, only with the gun receipt dealers flying in from another direction. It was evident that these men had only recently begun frequenting the island. The receipt dealers added one sentence when they recited their litany: they said, "You are brave fighters against imperialism; remember in your struggle the horror of capitalist oppression." A final voice came and announced, This is the miracle of the planned economy. This is what they call socialism. This is the chief fuel for the engines of despair.

Upon returning from these visions I paid my tutor an extra ten bucks.

And beat it out of there pronto.

DILIGENT Historians...

DILIGENT Historians have suffered in the past... and they're suffering now. Those apprised of the background data that makes up the whole of the Illuminati mythos are not surprised to hear that those who know too much sometimes find themselves being given a helping hand in the difficult crossover to the world beyond. But of late, a new rash of disappearances, hushed up of course, has brought underground attention to the studies conducted under the aegis of the Assassination Society of America.

The Society, organized back in the dark years before NSA bugs and moles could pierce any veil of mystery, originally romanticized the lonely hero with a knife. Members kept to themselves and collected impressive weapons stores, and as they aged, took respectable positions in many key socio-economic niches throughout the more advanced sectors of the American landscape.

Of late, however, and only with difficulty, it has been established that the sudden, unexplained departure of many prominent citizens throughout the land is the work of some sinister conspiracy. It seems that subtle clues were left that indicated that members of the Assassination Society, inactive though it may be, are the target of a quiet mop-up campaign. Why?

It is well known that certain scholarly research institutes, among them the Center for Libertarian Studies and the CATO Institute; plus their less-academically respectable associates in the Ultra-faction of the MLL, are entirely funded and controlled by ASA members. Recently, startling evidence of a centuries-old conspiracy has been unveiled and popularly promulgated by the aforementioned Libertarian fronts. The conspiracy originally declared that it was devoted to world domination through the use of dynamite, and though as time went on it moved on to bigger and better tools that depended on Uranium or its cousins, it has never once retreated or suffered a setback. The conspiracy counts among its devotees every member of every political party that has ever existed, and then some. It need hardly be added that the conspiracy long ago realized its goal, to cover the planet with governments, but unfortunate members of the ASA foolishly thought it safe to reveal their knowledge.

(Interruption)

The atmosphere boiled, astronauts were busy, X-boy fired his camera for future reference. At the astronauts; at the astronauts' headquarters they fired back, at random by our standards, striking us without plan but perhaps according to some one of their own.

Their vantage point is spectacular, which helps us; the glow—the heat let off by the wires—will obscure the view and accentuate larger, incorrect patterns, letting those who wish vanish into the void of interstices… But we fire away, too, knowing that our transmissions will be intercepted…

"You're lying," she told me, "stop a shaky frame bed." X-Boy was there too, for the guided fantasy therapeutics, our great hope: he of the wild database, the Assimilator, dreamer. Later we would wake from our session and be debriefed by our man, the photographer eideticist…

"Approaching you comes a young woman—she's got a chess board, heavy one, the pieces are set up for play… she props you up in your hospital bed, turns the crank raising you on your dais and sets up the board now so you can reach it."

I heard the change in breathing that meant one of our number had already gone down, been bitten. Struggled to maintain the visuals without forgetting myself; we had to remember. For later. What a bitch; they wouldn't torture us any more knowing how close we were, no, worse, let us lie there or bring us food, tend us carefully making small talk; we so weakened as not to be able to hate.

I played black, Alekhine's Defense to throw them

off…when they drained it out of me later they wouldn't be so sure I didn't do it to dump the game without being too obvious…X-Boy could win it, he's the last one left, it can't go on much longer.

The Opponent came on but with broken pawn center, foolish P-Q3 instead of P-K5…but we rallied more than our men, we rose up off our beds and forgot this game here. The young ladies stared at the boards flying up through the air and the naked wounded sheets aside climbing out. Too slow but the tactic bought us time.

PART TWO
(CERVANTES)

CRITICISM
POLEMICS
ESSAYS
SATIRE
POETRY

. . .

Publisher's Note

Drawn from correspondence with Bob Black and Denis McBee, "Post-Mortem" constitutes Gerry Reith's formal prepublication commentary on the original Neither/Nor Press edition of *Neutron Gun*, which included contributions by other writers that do not appear in this volume. Reith's remarks on material written by others—as well as his references to the story order—are preserved here not in the original spirit of a fragmentary afterword (that would be confusing), but for such metatextual insight that may be gleaned. The reader seeking originary context is advised to consult the first edition of *Neutron Gun*, or such facsimiles that may be found on the Internet.

Post-Mortem

First there is the raw—the raw emotion of ballsy vandals who not only broke into the temple and stole the silver, but melted it down and made better, more beautiful things.

We intend to show that our contempt for the rotted culture we vandalize is justified by our superior ability; and it is an afterthought that the whole work is colored by the disgust and despair of incidentally being trapped within a global totalitarian culture.

(The struggle is not as I thought it was, between the damned-if-do-or-don't bureaucratization or economization of social relations. No. These are like right and left, twin straw men who distract us while the real demon encroaches…no, revels in having succeeded at subduing us…trivialization. The sideshow of bureaucracy vs. economy only serves the end of trivializing us.)

In particular we have the following specific complaints reiterated:

Carly (Sommerstein) takes consumerism to task by doing a vignette in which her main allegorical cypher dies of an overdose of vaginal douche.

Ed (Lawrence) rants and moans in a pervasive style about the technological style that pervades our culture ("culture" for lack of a better word). He sneers at and smears a series of manifestations of the underlying theme in AMERICA: for instance, the supercession of carbon life forms by silicon...and the advocates of this.

"Gregor (Tomc) joyously draws mustaches on what are admittedly no longer sacred cows anywhere but in Eastern European hierarchies: first Marx and Engels, then Lenin and Stalin, and finally Enver Hoxha. He does it by writing pornography about them, in ever more repellent development. It works as a generic smear of the totemist left, however, and it is pure fun, aside from expressing a real disgust through the use of base metaphor...

"Bob (Black)'s introduction is intentionally ambiguous and also serves as a satire on modernist critical pretension. He manages, however, to master the kind of "field of play" stuff that a lot of modernist literary hacks get off on, and inserts some real advocacy by first setting up and then demolishing (in the sparest possible cases against X,Y,Z) Marxism, Christianity, liberalism, etc., and then issuing a very stark challenge... "Serfs Up!" He also ridicules the author-editor, me, in a few subtle points, but that's definitely consistent...

So far everything has contained, as well, an intentional taint of cheapness which is secretly false, if you follow, as in the theory of BullDaDa according to Doug

Smith (The Church of the SubGenius). If we're going to laugh, or make them think were laughing, at the bullshit we parody, then we have to trick them into having to decide whether we really are or not, by giving them apparently CHEAP work which is, upon closer inspection, tight and good.

This reinforces the theme which I establish independently, which is to bludgeon the reader with the problem of WHAT HE'S GOING TO DO WITH HIS LIFE, by overuse of the analogical literary problem of WHO'S DOING THE INTERPRETING HERE. In modern literary scholarship (in academia) a debate rages over the possible modes of interpretation, with the faction that would banish the author's intentions currently holding the upper hand. All the conflicts in possible interpretation lead back to the supereminent question of whether or not the author is going to be allowed to mean what he means…whether the self-indulgent reader is going to let himself off the hook by a corrupt doctrine that denies objective communication. We use the theme over and over, and I do it in almost every piece…it is reinforced on a subtler plane with struts that virtually FORCE the reader to ENGAGE, to make a choice, to take an active role. (In video media, the viewer is essentially passive.)

This is the key to understanding where the corrupt modernists make fools of themselves: in that they keep missing the point. In Pynchon, for instance, that by giving the reader an incredible, incredibly wide "field of play" we demand that he take an active role, which is like about as obvious as you can get in the task telling them nicely that YOU MOTHERFUCKERS HAVE GOT TO CONCEIVE OF THIS PROJECT AS ONE OF REAL HUMAN ACTIVITY AND THEREFORE, ERGO, ONE WHERE THE AUTHOR IS—and can be—SAYING SOMETHING MEANINGFUL, etc. etc. I must reword this. When they are presented with the choice it is made obvious that they must choose. That they must choose is final proof of—even if only in minimal—the author's autonomy and control over the Text of the text, and it is a metafictional comment on the decay of the age that we must resort to such cheap tactics in order to deal with our degenerate audience of educated but pusillanimous critics.

All by way of leading back, since: remember, this is, this whole little literary debate is a metaphor, to the question of what to do with your life. It is resonance, this bit about choosing, engaging, and who's going to be autonomous.

I think I will have been successful in making the connection. In particular, I portray a "passive reader" who is shot by a clown (the author) in what is scheduled to be the opening piece in the book. The theme is established, then: we're tired of and disgusted with passivity and we hardly think that reading is going to do anything to cure it but this is one last try.

In one piece I subtly comment on the destruction of the person that results from economization: "Fraud, Cheat, Lie, Thrill" is chock full of RIP-OFF and prostitution and loss, and emptiness. As a twist for the cognoscenti the piece itself will initially give its reader the feeling of having been ripped off I hope and expect. Richard Miller (Sun Tzu) has one in which he baits the Jews and advocates assassination of mealy-mouthed religious leaders, to the effect that this is an avenue worth exploring in our quest for a life worth living.

In another piece I deliver what I hope is a powerful little diagram of the three typical responses to State Power, along with an implied critical stance toward all of them, with the drawback that it does not end on an upbeat note, does not give as an avenue out.

In "Foreign Policy" I make a very subtle comment on the relations between the superpowers and the third world, but it is mainly cast in terms of a perverse and unpleasant dialogue between painfully intimate individuals, the narrator being extremely unsympathetic up until the last word, and even then somewhat repellent, though necessarily to drive home the point he makes against hierarchical, bureaucratized relationships. He's shown participating in one, and then objecting, so since he has to be a participant in order to KNOW what is wrong, and since he couldn't be a credible participant unless he committed the sins and follies of it, he is like a guy who wakes up at the end of a nightmare. We never fully get over our feeling that he is not yet cured. A teaser.

In "Johns Adventure" I do a delirious treatment of the Zerzanist vision, and of course unfairly smear it. We have a short, quick little dialectic with the agent living in a world where literally EVERYTHING is falling apart, and he begins to participate in the process, with not one minor suggestion that there is a possibility of some other form of action which would be better. He's really will-less even though he begins to kill, trash, etc. I don't know if maybe there shouldn't have been a contrasting figure who would show a will by refusing to harmonize with his environment,

But...that's moot now, and it is all so heavy that not one in a thousand will pick up on it enough to articulate this stuff the way I do. Hopefully they'll dimly sense it, which is all they ever do with anything and all I ever do with anything that I didn't sweat over myself.

And finally, "Twilight To Authority," [which] goes nicely as the end piece, the final note, the closing shot. This is because—aside from being a love song, a suicide note, an anarchist lament, PLUS a comment on any and every possible difficult decision. PLUS the pure abstraction of a structure like a chess game—it is also a modernist self-referential metafiction which comments on the relations between author and reader, as well as detourning itself by BEING THE STORY THAT IS ABOUT HOW IT WILL BE READ, and the STORY

THAT ASSUMES IT IS BEING ADDRESSED BY THE AUTHOR, and several other tricky changes.

The critical line for this interpretive magic is: "Now, inexplicably, the eyes had turned." It is there that the person-tense shifts…Another clue: watch the time when the narrator turns from WE to YOU. It is a tight little gem, which in the context of the book will also turn out to be a comment on how the book itself is read, as well as being, simultaneously, an address to the book.

It will be fun, if we get any critical notice, to see to what extent the critics are able to pick up on all this. It is very obvious. and yet…

Art Rant

Whatever brings in the most money for the least effort is art. All the rest is bad art or industrial aids. Of course, artists have managed to make many things difficult for themselves, but this is just a ploy to keep the scam from becoming perfectly clear to the investors.

Most people know there's something fishy about it all, but some of the pictures (or whatever) actually turn out to be attractive to at least a few among the population at large, so they don't worry too much about it if someone else buys stupid art and puts it in museums and so on.

The investors make sure that only the most neurotically picky make it as critics, because if anything else was the case then it would be hard to staunch the flow and pretty soon nobody would know which was the best art. Everyone would have to pick what they liked if they wanted to have something. The investment potential would be shot. All kinds of good amateurs might sweep aside the poseurs who bring in the dough.

Critics are taken in by The Line. Artists have to present the skeleton of a Theory which is fleshed out by critics, and turned into a Movement. The Line has all sorts of pseudo-philosophical and epistemological jargon mixed together like a tossed salad, and is quite often more engaging than any of the artworks that it is supposedly responsible for.

In essence, all of The Lines have one core statement. "Very few people," it says, "understand what this is all about." If you have gotten that far on your own, it means you have struggled with the divine jargon so long that you can toss it off at cocktail parties as facilely as the best of them. Being probably the most mystifying form of lies, The Line is a perfect mechanism for letting people believe themselves when they make stupid statements—not unlike religion and science. Sucked in because others, seemingly so capable, are also catering to the mouthings, one never realizes that all the trappings are empty, devoid of meaning, and that the only important part about it is the simple, direct communique concerning the number of people who are even qualified to talk about the subject. A strange Loop occurs. Like Zen, it is difficult to impart without engaging in the activity itself.

The perfect artwork, like the perfect money, has distilled The Line: all items have two values, broadly defined. They may have use value, or exchange value, or both. The use value of money is restricted almost solely to its exchange value, especially in the case of government-issue fiat paper. Nothing more need be said at present. Art may have two values: appreciation and

mystification. The highest (or most valuable-as-invest-
ment) art achieves the total subjection of appreciation
into mystification. Hence it might seem that a canvas
proclaiming in, say, thirty-two point Century Old Style
type, "Very few people really understand what this is all
about," would be appropriate for a portfolio or the walls
of a museum.

When those on the outs succeed in proselytizing
and causing the uninitiated to make purchases of those
works which are not at present popular, we see an art
revolution, and we laugh last, all the way to the bank.

Science Fiction: Overrated

When I see people, especially those engaged in generating science fiction, touting it as The Literature of Ideas, I have to roll my eyes and ask myself whether these people can properly be called literate.

Anyone truly interested in a literature of ideas is advised to do a general survey of, for instance, Russian literature, which if it can lay claim to anything it is that it is founded on and dependent on ideas. Russian literature (and I'm talking mainly about that which grew before the October revolution with the exclusion perhaps of Solzhenitsyn and Zamistin) was written by, for, and about intelligent people in dire straits. The ideas and issues of the day got wide play…and were very important to those who read them. In comparison to just this branch of literature, Science Fiction is the idle pastime of dilettantes and camp followers, of popularizers, cranks, and enthusiasts with no convictions.

And I say in comparison because in fact every literature is concerned with ideas, is in fact a literature of ideas. In that sense, this calling any literature a literature of ideas is redundant. But in my view, the Sci-Fi aficionados are expressing an overcompensation, being a touch too defensive in response to previously non-existent questions about the whole endeavor.

I grew up in a home that had plenty of bookshelves in every room; and plenty of space was devoted to Sci-Fi. I had access to *Worlds of SF*, *Galaxy*, *F & SF*, *Amazing* and *Astounding*, and *Analog*, which magazine was represented practically in full since the famous name-change, including the rare 8 1/2" x 11" editions. The first thing I recall reading was a story in *Analog*, in fact. I have read most of the classics and plenty of the minor classics, but though I'm familiar with the field I have not stayed in contact enough lately to say that I am well-read in it.

If I am to pronounce judgment, which I dearly love to, I must say that Sci-Fi as a literature of ideas is largely a fraud. To those familiar with the other branches of literature, it is clear that in the case of science fiction, more often than not the genre is used primarily to force conclusions and convictions that the author would have great difficulty doing in another scenario. I am saying that Sci-Fi is too easy. You will find mountains of dated, tired propaganda in the field of science fiction, written by lightweights who got (and stayed) excited about this or that and then had to create an entirely new world in order to prove it or support it. By and large the science fiction that we like is the science fiction that expresses moral conclusions that we like. (For non-moralists, take the appropriate referent of your choice.) It is propaganda of the cheapest sort, demeaning and at times even insulting. For the most part it does not accelerate moral ambivalence or stress; it will not allow into the plots any characters any shade of doubt: all is black and white. There is hardly and meat there for the alert reader to grab onto and chew at, thinking things out. The symbolism likewise is tawdry and transparent. This stuff is for sleepers and those who lie in bed trying to go to sleep, written by the same kind.

The difference is that it takes a lot more work to make a statement or to produce a really comprehensive and honest appraisal of issues in other literatures. (I speak primarily of realist stuff, though I have a task for symbolist work.) In other literatures one is saddled with the problems of characters who are not one dimensional; of worlds in upheaval or uncertainty, of loose ends. With a stroke of the pen we can wipe away all this; we can create a new world that simply ignores critics, opposing views, deeper analysis that shows our flawed premises, and so on. Indeed, while a world is turning away, for instance, from regimentation, authoritarianism, hierarchy, and militarism (as expressed in the classics), we find all of these things in abundance in the glittering spectacles of the Sci-Fi Masters, who drool and squirm in delight at having done away with all the nasty problems.

In science fiction the need is to be able to heavy-handedly abolish those same challenges to authority and force; that the authors of this obnoxious literature must leave the realms of reality as but an indicator of their abject puerility, their sterility and impotence at answering, or constructing, a world view that comes to their preferred conclusions without sacrificing honesty.

Now, I am not saying that I dislike science fiction. I actually like it, in small doses and select. But I am tired of potato chips and pop; I grew up on them, malnourished, and have been eating a healthy diet for years.

And to defray, offset some of the fire earlier, I must allow certain things. For one, I do not condemn the entire field; just as there are hacks rampant, a few shining stars of capability and strength make appearances. Just as some of these same despicable lazy hacks worship authority, god, home, apple pie, senators, technology and mom (not to mention flag, virginity, baseball and hot dogs and like maudlin trifles cynically abused), there are those who brave the winds of a slavering bootlicking audience and actually write novels and stories willing to call these things to the bar of justice. And just as there are gems to be found on the Other Shelves at the bookstore, immense shelf space is spent purveying the lightest tripe, the sickest and sickliest junk. Each of my charges is balanced in that there are those who do not so sin.

What, then, is the charge? Of what is the defendant accused? We accuse him of being an overrated product, a puff sold by fanatics with shining eyes, a grisly humorless body of work devoted in the main to the worst in our national culture. When illiterates like Sam Konkin "write" in their pamphlets that they have found the literature of libertarianism I must spit. What he is saying is that he hasn't paid the slightest attention to the actual nature of this retrograde industry and that he wants to leap on the bandwagon of people who confirm that this "literature" is naught but a cheap propaganda. Now, overrated. The crime is identified, if not applicable to call in some sort of class action suit in reverse. What I want is to put my readers on warning that no longer will they get away with mouthings to the effect that science fiction is the literature of ideas. Imagine! The gall of it! What utter tosh!

Any takers?

Quixote: How to Use

> "How the devil can we take revenge," replied Sancho, "when there are more than twenty of them, and we are only two—or perhaps no more than one and a half?"
>
> "I am equal to a hundred," answered Don Quixote. Then without further discussion he drew his sword and attacked the Yanguesans; and Sancho was spurred on by his master's example to do the same.
>
> (*Part One, Chapter XV*)

In the culture of planned obsolescence where no work avoids seeming dated within weeks of its introduction Quixote occupies a curious place. It ought surprise us that he has been revised and rewritten more than any other figure in modern literature; because this cannot simply indicate some profound universality. Innumerable less sparkling versions hand us a new mediation: the superficial literal figure denuded in revealing ways; the pathetic old man whose delusion we with pretension deign to enjoy. As with all spectacles his *real misadventure* begs the question of our *false adventures*.

Feeling a lack we take his story for jolly wordplay and station ourselves above it like the fatuous adult who takes vacations and on occasion envies the child.

The condescending words of one translator indicate this. "…and even in his most preposterous battles… " says that dunce of a doorman, "…(he) always has our loving sympathy." It should be the other way around. Quixote is free and we are the slaves; we are the ones who deserve pity and sympathy. But Cervantes is too wily for that, and in order to escape the necessary conclusions we construct ourselves as tough realists who bear the weight on our shoulders; the banality of everyday life, the misery of our submission. Thus it is that we see in Quixote the brief respite of comic relief. His message is infinitely more dangerous but we are given grace because he could not control his revisionists.

Quixote is taken as the standard to which all other futilities must be must be compared and found wanting. This in itself ought to give the perceptive a moment's pause; but we are wrong to continue in our simplicity about it. Treating him as something like the greatest or most abject of losers is just another attractive inaccuracy in our attempt to sidestep the issue.

They key, of course, is that he is never *abject*. Later in the story above, Quixote and Sancho are both roundly trounced; but Quixote at least is not sorry. (Sancho's repentance is necessary. He *is not* really a squire but a reflection of the ideal reader: an understandably reluctant apprentice.) I am reminded of an event in my own life: once when offered an early morning beer a friend of mine considered and then rejected the offer, saying, "No, when you drink in the morning it is a sign of problems." And what can we say when this is the *only reason to refuse*? Here is the abject. The greatest thing about Quixote is that he never learns his lesson. It should hardly need be added that this is a double boon: he is also spared the learning of the wrong lessons.

The difference between Quixote and Sisyphus gives us more clues. Start with the given conditions and it is clear that Sisyphus' story was meant (at least in Camus' mediation) to be a point by point real life analogue. The sickly melodrama, the pall, tell us that its sculptor well those passions read which yet survive, stamped on these lifeless things. He believed it, took it seriously; the very force of the supereminent abstractions to which Sisyphus is condemned tell us that Camus was trying to argue his way past a door that he didn't know wasn't locked. No fundamentals are called into question and the real breakdown of reductionism is never even approached. Thus trapped by self imposed bars he had to create Sisyphus as triumphant though arrogance. "There is no fate that cannot be surmounted by scorn." This is true for the situation but ultimately unnecessary. Scorn will always be overcompensation.

The other vital distinction is that while Sisyphus is self-conscious, Quixote is not. (At least for now this must be left imprecise; suffice to say that he does not share the awareness of himself as vain struggler that marks the follower of Sisyphus.) This lack of self consciousness is not *only* explained by suggesting that the parodic framework would be compromised and not *only* dissolved by seeing that the character Quixote would be paralyzed. It is because the Sisyphus model is fundamentally in error that his self consciousness becomes necessary. This is not meant to deny the role of reflexivity but to maintain that the differing forms are mutually exclusive and that the one, namely that found in Sisyphus, is false. A way out of the wilderness can only be indicated here since my maps are not complete: Quixote, though ostensibly a direct parody, was not; and thus he was never a direct character either. "I know who I am," replied Don Quixote, "and I know, too, that I am capable of being not only the characters I have named, but all the Twelve Peers of France and all the Nine Worthies as well…"

Now what? We must remake our lives; and not only because we cannot avoid doing so. The bars being as often as not on the inside it is time to follow the knight's example and place emphasis on the other end of the ancient libratory formula: "Look before you leap; he who hesitates is lost." "It is quite clear," replied Don Quixote, "that you are not experienced in this matter of adventures. They are giants, and if you are afraid, go away and say your prayers…"

"I have done, am doing, and shall do the most famous deeds of chivalry that the world has ever seen, can see or will see." In the end we are all Quixote; what we forget too often is that we are also Cervantes.

> Come, my friends, 'tis not too late to seek a newer world. Push off, and setting well in order smite the sounding furrows; for my purpose holds to sail beyond the sunset, and the baths of all the western stars…
>
> — *Ulysses* (Tennyson)

Manifesto Notes, 1

Beginnings are not analytical; reflections are, and reflections come after the fact. To open by proposing to start at the beginning, then, would be pointless, in the first place because it would be impossible, and in the second because to do anything other than to open with the abstract would be to compromise one's goal of starting with the beginning. One cannot ever start at the beginning, but every start is the beginning; one cannot avoid starting at the beginning.

An emotion, then.

I despise senior citizens. I hold an immutable, deep, and abiding distrust and suspicion of them in general. I work at a motel, answering phones and the like. Early one morning I got a call from one room, it was one ancient lady with quavering voice asking directions to the hospital.

Alarmed and eager to help, I asked, "Oh! Do you need an ambulance?"

The response was irritated and vague, impossible to interpret. "No, no."

"Can I get you a cab, then?" My worry was not the less

real because it was cultivated for my job's sake.

Again the irritation. "I don't want a cab!" the old bitch said, and hung up. I heard nothing more.

Until a few weeks ago, probably three months after the incident. I was passing the desk on my way to have a cup of coffee, it was the change of shift, all my workmates were there and my bosses. "Hey, Gerry," called Tim, the senior clerk.

"Yes?" I asked.

"Do you remember a call from someone asking directions to the hospital? Early in the morning?"

The context was always a few days when someone asked me if I recalled this or that event at work; I cannot think of a situation where there has been a longer period. No connection.

"No," I asked, "Why?"

"Well, we got a postcard from someone who says they stayed here and they called in the morning asking directions to the hospital and they said the desk clerk told them they had to get an ambulance."

"Ah," I said, not knowing what was appropriate. No connection, no guilt, what's the point. I didn't do it. In fact I felt relieved, since it was clear that they had been discussing the matter and had come to the consensus that while none of them was culpable, a Crime had been committed.

Sharon tittered. "At the bottom they wrote 'Would you please fire that desk clerk!'; it was an old lady in AARP."

Still nothing. "Where's the card," I asked, interested, curious, involved but not involved, feeling that there was a point being made to me by those assembled judges but not getting the point. Most blameless am I.

"It's in the office, that's where it belongs," says one boss, a friend who suddenly has a gruff demeanor. What, I think, is this? All eyes are upon me for the tribunal, I didn't do anything, what's it all about, why, Brent, are you so gruff, do you think I intended to tear up Exhibit A or something? This mention of job-loss has me all upset.

"No," I say, "I don't recall anything like that… " And I didn't! But there is nothing I can say!

Minutes later the event dawns on me, minutes too late to go back and say, yes, I recall having spoken about the hospital with an old lady; because it will sound like I am adjusting the truth to both admit involvement and exculpate myself at the same time. Sneaky, and their conclusion? Why doesn't he admit to it, then? and perhaps promise not to do it again?

My friends, eying me! Work is a formal matter, yes, I know better than all of you assembled: none of you has spent your last dollar, not once in your entire easy lives; not one of you has been on the road with nothing, and with no one to call upon for aid. Above all the gravity of the situation is clear to me, yes! AARP complaints can mean bad business, and that too can threaten me directly. You fools!

But the real object of my ire was the lying elder. The invidious worm of a stupid old shit who would do something like that! What, menopause? What, a bad day at the races? And take it out on someone a thousand miles away because you have a moment's power and influence? Your uncreative brain being too sterile with age to come up with cleverer, local persecutions, you must confine yourself to half-real events? Oh, painful death upon you! Cut off your blood money Social Security checks: I rage to think my FICA payments go out to stuff the debased mouths of these walking intestinal tracts, I would let you starve in the streets without a moment's fleeting sense of shame, guilt, compassion. I hate you, and I will never forgive.

And so I was implicated, charged with an offense I didn't commit but which I can never disprove; my trial was conducted in secret without my presence, the verdict handed down from on high with no appeals possible. All in the lies and calumny of someone I will never see again; all in the devolved mind of a scum-brained bag of bones that lived longer than was just. I offer up Kafka, who can take it with a grain of salt and a knowing, cynical smile. But as for me, I cannot brook being under the power of nameless, absurd enemies. Enemies, fine, but honest ones. The matter weighs heavily, I cannot ever forget. Telling it to this, the powerless court of public opinion, consoles, and it gives power to another project. Done.

On Factsheet Five

The mystery of SF fandom's eternal obscurity is easily solved by taking a look at some of its members' work. While Mike Gunderloy may not be a fully-qualified boot-lapper, he certainly aspires to it considering the praise he heaps on those, deeper in the cult, mentioned in his disgusting quarterly, *Factsheet Five*.

Factsheet Five is supposedly intended to serve as a useful function by publicizing the work of others. From the start we see the sterility of the project: whereas newspapers in the modern age are little more than advertising circulars with a few random and trivial facts thrown in to hold the reader's interest and induce him to turn the pages, here we have the circular itself, pure, standing alone.

And what does he purvey? We have a selection of anarchist newsletters, some good, some not; the self-published work of a number of understandably obscure artists—understandably not in that I presume to judge that which I haven't seen, but in that they are young and make the mistake of associating with Gunderloy-types—...and a few book reviews that are more an attempt to keep the reader well-aware that Mr. G reads a lot, a lot of the correct stuff, than anything else.

Lately he has gotten others to join him in his reviewing dabbles; none of them distinguished for their ability to make up their mind or say anything with any flair. Anni Ackner stands out, but offensively so: while she shows signs of style, it is overdone, so far as to become vile. Her angle is cuteness and clever turn-of-phrase; and as they say, brevity is the soul of wit. Alone among them I forgive her and grant indulgence in hopes that someone will pass on this single recommendation: *learn to cut*. She may redeem herself.

The rest inspire actual loathing. Those misfortunate enough to earn a listing with FF have to be imagined as victims of chagrin or mild distaste...either that or stupid...because no matter what it is, no exceptions allowed, Gunderloy and his crew manage in their tired two sentence assessment to denigrate it. Not a single thing mentioned in their little list is not followed with some disclaimer to the effect that "it's okay if you like that kind of stuff," or, "real weird, kiddies." Somehow it comes off as an unintentional masterpiece: here is a promoter who spoils everything he touches! As if to detour promotion, he spits on everything deemed worthy of mention; what makes it beautiful is that he doesn't seem to realize it.

Despite the puerile off-handed and strainedly-relaxed pose that Gunderloy takes, the one that provokes him to say that *FF* is a review of the stuff that appears in his mailbox, we detect a unifying theme: that of the quest for entertainment-value. Gunderloy is promoting obscurity and unusualness in the arts and in politics; he hopes to find something strange enough to hold his interest for more than a minute.

And this is why he is doomed to failure. The connoisseur, jaded, is still going to appreciate things for what they are. He doesn't. He is too dull; too much concerned with finding fashionably deviant material to wave around and secure for himself credentials as an "Underground Contactee." He'll always be bored with it all, because the only use he gets from art is titillation, and the only use he has for political doctrine resembles a straight man for snide, uncomprehending comments. Not a single thing there seems to provoke a reflection from him more profound than that the item in question "may go somewhere,"—as with a political group; or that it is "worth the price." Some reviews!

Worse: he has no opinion, not even one he values enough to stand up for. This means he will of course remain uninformed, willfully ignorant, and that he will grant no respect to the ideas of others. A writer so lacking in ability worth being proud of, or ideas worth arguing about, cannot be of much use to the reader. He comes off as a pompous, condescending, patronizing phony; he won't commit himself to anything, and we begin to see the disparate entries not so much as an exemplary refusal to be politically-blinkered as an inability to make up his own mind about anything. The listees are all sold-out, mediated, cheaply described in terms of their value to intellectual masturbator of the western world...number 857,622. To be contemplated by Gunderloy is to be insulted.

A fraud. He can't or won't make up his mind about anything; he is quick to deliver the sneering line that—unknown to him—fails to answer those who pose a threat by standing for something; he can't write; is bored with reading; yet he keeps it up. And for what? To associate himself with... to snuggle up next to, people whom he dimly perceives as having something he doesn't. This is the essence of fandom, and we can be thankful that it won't spread far; only in science fiction circles dominated by theorists of open, heavy hierarchy, is it tolerated and encouraged, this pusillanimous fawning.

On *Processed World*

What distinguishes *Processed World* is the amazement it instills in the educated reader, i.e. in how close and yet so far. The whole thing is tantalizing, clearly the product of people who have at least one finger on the pulse. The rest must be in their noses. They remind me of myself: someone who has in the past successfully battled his way out of paper bags and become convinced that there is nothing more to be learned. What a shock when you remember that you don't know it at all! But this shock is not part of the correspondence, as the people responsible for *PW* seem not to have challenged a single one of their premises, or their own methods, since 1968. Dressed up in chic print, chic format—a magazine!—for the disaffected!—cute style—changing ink! how novel!—but does it redeem?—we recall French cooking of the middle ages that developed ever more complex spicing to compensate for rotted meat, game flesh. A slight redolence of decay pervades when the taste buds have grown accustomed to the spice, it peeks through once again the ignorance is just as thick.

Tom Euthanasia babbles about capital, information, industry, and the world economy without one single thought in his head beyond the unshakable conviction that since he thinks about such matters, he's qualified to pass judgment on them. Whence cometh this feeling that the editors are completely competent—let alone morally justified!—in exercising control over the entire world? The only objection they seem to think worthy of consideration is the one to the effect that they lack personnel and this is the whole point of *PW*: recruitment! The absurd arrogance is what will make this item a boon for future collectors and historians of the ridiculous and failed.

Of course, when they appear to approach consciousness of this contradiction, they roll out the "direct democracy" artillery, or this absurd councilism. They never face the contradiction that this produces: assuming global planning in accordance with their visions of propriety, how do we integrate the will of the councils? Do we assume they all agree with us? Or do we face the hell of competing world economy, a hideous free market, free of our control? They can worship computers forever, but they will never be enabled to plan any economy above the level of a small business—this being the source of their fervid, if soft-pedaled, anti-bourgeois sentiment—because even were you able to marshal all relevant data (and you cannot) your data communications devices are no substitute for judgment. People have always made errors even with all the relevant information at their fingertips, which is the bane of central authority and the luck of the lowly individual; it is a new conceit to think that a with a fresh word processor in front of you, you are able to be wise. Garbage in, garbage out. Humans are doing the input as well you know. Who are the anti-human here? The ones who do not aspire to control, or the ones who do so aspire, but trust themselves so little that they make a fetish of machines as a substitute for choosing?

Bad Company: *Oath of Fealty*

Science Fiction writers form the tightest and most messianic propagandist clique since the Scholastics, with whom they have much in common. Like beating dead horses, mistaking trivia for profundity, cavalier views on the rights of lesser men, and some bizarre notions of propriety.

Oath of Fealty* is more evidence of it. It is nothing more or less than an easy rewrite of *Lucifer's Hammer*; once again we see the same Science Fiction themes: technology-as-savior; hierarchy and rigid social structure as positively attractive; the Enemy so well-smeared so as to deserve sympathy from Satan. Bigotry is bad when it is perceived among the fence-sitters of the outright enemy, but there is nothing wrong with it when we do it.

Niven and Pournelle have churned out another action-packed thriller of no consequence, taking pains not to hide their prejudices behind any pantywaist proofs that one side or another is correct. First they steal

---
* *Oath of Fealty*, by Larry Niven and Jerry Pournelle, Phantasia Press (1981).

the idea of the Proprietary Community for an obscure group of futurist libertarians; it entails a city within a single building run with a soft iron hand by the owners, who have solid contracts with their residents. The owners and administrators provide a valuable commodity in this horror future: security. They have surveillance cameras everywhere; guards who watch everything, and special passes to keep out undesirables.

The conflict entails a plot by various conveniently rabid and violent environmentalists to destroy the big, private city. They're going to sneak in and blow up the power lines; they're going to use dynamite on the turbines and flywheels far underground. We see two attacks; the first turns out to be a prank by innocent youths who get gassed with some nerve poison. Because one of the youths was the son of a prominent politician on the Outside, tensions mount, and the man who pushed the button is arrested and jailed. With love affairs in the background we move ahead meeting everyone and finding out what's so wonderful about living in a friendly police state. Finally another attack is mounted, this one for real, and our anguished leaders do their best to capture the intruders without…the later confusion the jailed hero is rescued; an economic war is declared between the two cities and the Proprietary Community wins with threats and scare-tactics.

For structure the novel is not bad; although he characters are unidimensional we are only asked to swallow a few impossible motives and actions. If you enjoy thrillers, or exploring moral issues of some possible worlds, the book is worth the price.

But I have a problem with Niven, Pournelle, & Co.'s vision. Like any science fiction writer of renown barring but a few, they are on the Far Right, in the Pro-tech faction: conservatives in the worst sense. They are naive about power, even though they do heave in a quote from some Lord Acton imitator about its effects. The unease starts perhaps in *Lucifer's Hammer*, where the only group opposed to the Champions of Truth, Justice and Authority is a ragtag band of cannibals, environmentalists, and Christian cultists. Worse: they are largely black, and from the inner cities. It is almost the same in *Oath*: the savage, violent madmen with bombs; anyone who expresses some qualm about living in the Hive, as it is called, are bigots, Know-Nothings, or maniacs. The Heroes, the Good Guys, are obedient in the face of "duly constituted" authority: this authority is omniscient (in *Oath* they get brain implants that hook them up to the omniscient computer), benevolent, and wise beyond measure.

It becomes positively obnoxious when Niven and Pournelle start tossing around libertarian arguments for that section of their audience. Oh, it is clear: no one's rights are being violated except for the actions of the despicable Enemy; all the residents freely chose to live in the techno-feudal slave camp of the future; commerce is voluntary; the benefits are real. For instance, the city has negotiated a bargain that exempts all its people from filing taxes with any government; taxes are paid to some distant American state, and it comes out of the price of the rent.

It becomes clear that Niven and Pournelle (and many if not most of their fellow propagandists) are libertarians only to the extent that they could use freedom of association to create rigid, intolerant hierarchies; incredible class divisions; and the New Militarist Man. Reagan and ray-guns to the end of the galaxy; the more things change the more they keep telling us that they stay the same. Bob Black put his finger on it: "Everything can be different in the same old way! Less taxes, more rent! Less cops, more Pinkertons!"

Hero worship, slavish obedience, modernist hierarchies, and pure power are not libertarian, despite Ayn Rand and despite freely chosen submission. Contract or no contract we are talking about lockstep, lock-up, and lock-out. It is not libertarian to praise universal and inescapable surveillance no matter who wants it at what price and for what reason. To say that Niven and Pournelle are even faintly libertarian is to say that Pol Pot could be a Party member because everyone who saw what he was going to do had a chance to leave before he did it.

I am not one to prevent people from signing on with whatever dictatorial or discipline-oriented outfit they choose. Think of it is evolution in action as the novel's obscene slogan goes. If people want to follow Jim Jones to Guyana, or Sun Myung Moon to blissful flower dispensaries, that is their business.

But I do have a valid objection to propaganda that lauds such behavior. *Oath* does not really celebrate anything worth celebrating; they put Power on a pedestal, scorning present governments in favor of their own, in which there is no possibility that any action of the State can ever be challenged or impeded; in which it is never questioned and conveniently never wrong. *Oath* creates insipid people in a mutual admiration society; they're all Heroes because they obey the Boss; they fight only that authority which seems to get in their way; but have no qualms about being dictator. The obvious nature of relationships in brutal subcultures is glossed over: no more are the simpering, bootlicking weaklings who turn cruel tyrant even in evidence; no, authority is mediated, low-key, and no one in power ever pulls rank, revels in power, or does anything that the dominant/submissive psychotic tends to do.

People who like this milieu, who enjoy living sans dignity and autonomy, who pretend that submission isn't the watchword in hierarchies, are writing books in favor of it; and they're lauded by too many infantile libertarians. They seize on the few recognizable libertarian sentiments and skirt the glorification of Power. In the end of Niven and Pournelle's ode to dominance, the Perfect Leaders decide not to use their utter immunity and kill their helpless captives; anyone, anyone who takes this as an accurate projection of behavior, given history, cannot call themselves literate or informed, and anyone who thinks that this book even approaches a treatment of libertarian ethics is an absurd, ahistorical quack.

Libertarians who do not take a positive stance in favor of a tolerant ideal in various cultural and interpersonal codes do themselves grievous harm. All around us there are insidious preachers of the exact opposite of what we stand for stealing our arguments and foisting off their garbage on an unsuspecting public. If these ostensible freedom-lovers are not exposed, and opposed by a positive alternative ethic, we will end up being lumped together with all those who are rightly mistrusted by the independent-minded. Apologists for Power are bad company, and if we don't watch out, correct prejudice against them will destroy us.

Communication...

... First I would like to concern myself with the point at which communication breaks down. The experience that occurs when one makes the discovery that someone to whom expressions are directed will invariably misinterpret them...or behave in a way that is unexpected and/or less than pleasing.

But what is communication? It is the sharing or trading of an idea. In every situation that involves two or more living organisms conscious of each other's existence or proximity, communication occurs. Meanings are demonstrated and response to them is generated in the form of further demonstrated meanings.

This would all be very simple were it not for the situations we find ourselves in when information flow is interrupted, when we have insufficient data. In decisions, data is weighed and value is assigned to each variable. But when the unknowns are assigned value exceeding that of the available data, decision must be postponed until either 1) more data becomes available, or 2) reevaluation is complete.

This illustration shows the steps involved.*

Now that that's cleared up (or is it? ...more data... no new data...), we can move on to the original question.

Communication is when the Other becomes a data-source, as in box "Data input." As an element of the environment, some living organism is the source of data, or signals, that earn a value rating of over nil.

Now, the Other is going to be considering this as well. Whether we are intentionally directing signals toward another or not, our actions will be perceived and interpreted and rated in importance.

Communication breakdown is when you become exasperated and end up saying, "I can't explain it to you!" and you know that the other person, who has not been following, will conclude from this that whatever it was you were trying to say had no value anyway; when they say to themselves in response, "That doesn't make sense," and you realize that you have not even been able to communicate the sense of urgency that you felt about the matter, let alone the substance that elicited the urgent reactions.

---

* Graphic not available. –Ed.

An Introduction to SubGenius Theology: Brief Examinations of Several Doctrinal Points.
By H.P. of the U, G.B. Reith

Depending on your level of activity in the Church, doctrine plays an increasing role. In truth as well as practice, every single member of the Church represents a unique faction or schizm. "Bob" approves. But should the individual member find himself or herself wending his or her way deeper into the higher, hidden and arcane orders of the Church, with their complex, bizarre, and totalitarian belief systems, it becomes crystal clear that skill at Bobthink (dealing with finer theological points and being able to resolve in one's mind unresolvable opposites) is necessary. Indeed, many of "Bob's" most promising slavstudents have gone astray at juncture this very. Critical needless to say.

Should my reader at this point need review conceptual tools and Church structural underpinnings such as Bobthink, the eternally retractable statement of absolute truth, the constantly inventable doctrine, and related points such as the *shordurpersav*, the Supreme, Divine Fallibility of "Bob," and so on, consult your pamphlet. For now we can safely assume you are prepared this data for. Onward then.

The Two Conspiracies Theory.

Some think that there are actually two Conspiracies; this is known as the dualcy heresy. Representatives of this schizmatic cult will attempt to convince you that the Conspiracy is actually divided into two opposing camps whose only cooperation lies in not revealing their enmity so that the Normals won't suspect anything.

"Bob" shows us that this heresy is unfortunate but not pivotal. He lets us know that they are both one and the same. He points out that it is much akin to the error of the Eastern Cultists who war over perception of the world as either the Ping-Pong *split* or the Dow Chem *whole*. Anyway, it is both, and sometimes Conspiracy members will attempt to recruit you, explaining how evil the "other side" is. Don't be fooled. They will never let you really join and instead will simply use you as a pawn.

"Bob"'s Role in the Hierarchy.

This is relatively easy. Only the most Normal of the schizmatics have any doubts concerning "Bob's" role.

"Bob" is never to be questioned. Whatever "Bob" says is true, and whatever is attributed to "Bob" is true. If a conflict appears, it is not really a conflict. Sometimes "Bob" will make himself appear in visions to the unfaithful, convincing them to make stupid, blatant power plays or attempts to corrupt Church doctrine. He does this so that they will be exposed as wreckers.

"Bob" generally prevents people from lying about him unless he wants them to. The media, for instance, cannot help but lie about "Bob" and distort the Church whenever they report on it. This actually helps us . . . makes us more "slippery."

The Conspiracy-to-Normal Responsibility Ratio
New members tend to go overboard in placing the blame on the Conspiracy. Soon they learn of the major role played by its dupes—the Pinks, the Normals, and the Mediocretins.

The question is mainly one of intent. Many schizms have been formed over this issue. Many see the Conspiracy as the only agent worth blaming and deny the importance of the spineless and directionless cattle who cannot have acted otherwise and are thus absolved.

As "Bob" says, "Think how dumb the average guy is. Well, by definition, half of them are dumber than that." If we take the humanoid "normative state" to be completely unrelated to such qualifiers as functionality, success, health, happiness,—indeed, if we assume that egalitarians are anything but the rankest imbeciles (excremeditate on the idea of pushy Normals trying to make everyone exactly Normal! "Bob" wants this to enrage you)—then it is clear that the Normal is marked by bovinity, banality, chronic stupidity, being at once incurious, lazy, dumb, fat, and bored, in a word incapable of achieving success in the universe were it not for the "heroic" efforts of Conspiracy dupes and collaborators who gain for their worth lower-level power seats and squeeze the embryonic Overmen, thus keeping them semi-permanently stunted, to provide enough to feed and clothe the mindless many. Thus it is seen that the role of the Normals is integral to the success of the Conspiracy, since if in any one place the slopeheaded industrialized simians are in a majority they tend to monopolize and create a stifling atmosphere, even at times banding together to attack the rare Overman who attains self-awareness sufficient to produce action; this role can in no way validly be denied its place in the register of the inexcusable and the criminal.

This does not downgrade the primacy of the Conspiracy's role in oppressing the Church. The Normals are deformed only by specific action of top level Conspiracy members.

The more easily frustrated among the Church membership tend to see action-appropriateness on these questions in terms of *gain*. Thus the signal importance cannot be overrated. Can the Normals be blamed for their obnoxious ignorance? Although they are part and parcel, albeit unaware, of the Conspiracy itself, can we plot their destruction since they are too shallow and empty minded to even suspect their gross idiocy? To the moron, everyone else is a moron; they cannot detect subtlety; the blind doubt the existence of sight. And since the Conspiracy is consciously directing its energy at the persecution of "Bob" and his Church, can we waste our time on the Normal wipeout project or should we go for the roots and watch the branches die later?

As tactical and strategic questions, the answers lie in the not-too-distant future when "Bob" has assembled sufficient data. It is not yet Bobclear that the Conspiracy can be defeated while the Normals maintain their inertial grip on culture and society. It is further theorized that more Conspiracies can spring up if the superstructure, a mass of blind robots, continues to exist, wandering around in a fog looking for strong leaders and national wills. Their sheer numbers are what counts, because they can be mobilized by television hypnotists among the Conspiracy top-cells even though they possess no thought of their own.

A subsidiary issue related to this one is the question of the division between *abolitionist* and *replacement* SubGenii. The replacementists urge direct war upon the Conspiracy with the express intent to smash and overthrow it. This they say will leave a gap which will be filled by the triumphant church members with "Bob" leading the way as a one man vanguard. They offer that although not very versatile, the Normals make pretty good servants, arguing that a worldwide reign of SubGenii presents no particular problem for the Church. As a matter of fact, not a single Church member sees anything wrong With this goal. Vengeance on the Normals who brought this mess can only be exacted by crushing their present masters and then replacing it with a reign of terror so vast and inescapable that not a peep will be raised in opposition by even the most popular and well known dissident scientists. It is our due for having been kept down for so long by the malicious and the ignorant and the apathetic. They don't care? Well, good, they won't care when we run the show either. Since we deserve pure power for our long suffering, it is our right and our duty to take it and abuse it.

The abolitionists make an amendment to this case by suggesting that although taking power is okay, since we don't want any of us to end up on the underside of the heap in the future, we must make sure to abolish the Normals as soon as we seize the wheel. Both the Conspiracy members and the Normals must meet nuclear evaporation to cleanse the planet. If this step is not taken, then potential further Conspiracies can develop among the ranks of the Church hierarchy, ruining our plan to establish a world of total joy-seeking abandon. Again, though, the answers to these questions lie in the future. "Bob" is carefully watching the laboratory in Cambodia for relevant data on the success of similar measures.

The Salvation Through Display Paradox

Only a Normal would understand that liberation starts at home. Throwing off the shackles of a Conspiracy created Normal-supported moral standard and stifling cultural milieu must be the first step in individual development. Run wild and do whatever the fuck you please and you are saved. If you cannot see that the Normals are the source of such pernicious diseases as original sin, and that they can only be erased by engaging in forbidden acts, then you are a Normal, and by special design this publication and everything in it was written and structured so that it appears to you to be only the most horrible and insane of infantile documents. Indeed, it is, but you cannot see why, or to what purpose besides those fed to you by the Conspiracy through its tentacles and tendrils in the Normal media as stock explanations suitable to justify dismissal from concern of all odd or disturbing events. Thus the contents of the publication are absolutely incomprehensible to you except as mere entertainment or, if you are slightly higher than most, as some sort of rough commentary on the state of things. In actuality this publication is a direct communication to secret Church members throughout the world. The Church has been underground for more than three thousand years now, and our lines of communication have been cut by the Conspiracy so we must resort to the most intricate of coded messages, allegories, symbol system manipulations, parodic lyricism, and metaphysical SubReference so that we can communicate directly with each other's minds without letting anyone else know what is going on. We admit all this to insure disbelief by all but the most laughable of paranoiacs, to whom nobody listens anyway. But all that *you* see is a perhaps ludicrous and sometimes repellent testimony concerning the debilitation of certain people. Really it is a very specific instruction manual filled with important data concerning matters that cannot be revealed. You see, the apparent Church truths are mixed with lies while we get the message across to those who count. Anyone who does take it seriously is in trouble. And this is the end of the Normal receptive portion of the magazine since the rest is too important to be revealed to the likes of you. Normals cannot be saved by "Bob," by the Church, or by any weirdness that they may be capable of contriving. Furthermore, many of the Normals reading this will think they are on the inside of a fashionable joke or some such tripe, and may smile or laugh or recommend it to others to demonstrate their hipness. Actually it is *they* who are the most rank of all, and who are the fullest and biggest brunt of any joke that this might be, since we have their money in *our* pockets. Any saving weirdness has to be authentic (something even the coolest of Normals cannot bear to work into their tight schedule of personae, for fear that they may alienate each other), and only true, natural SubGenii are able to commit real acts of strangeblat, weirdnoid, or releasistness.

The Problem in the Church Today: Its Resolution

The Church of the SubGenius is in obvious disarray. Faith in "Bob" wanes as the Hierarchites loudly proclaim its growth; contributions-flow fades to a dribble while these same men undertake vast new projects at a stunning rate. What has gone wrong, and how can we resolve the problems? To this question do I turn my attention in this essay; and woe be unto those at whom the fingers are pointed and the Stark Fists delivered: for it is no longer time for pussyfooting and friend-making. It is, in my opinion, too late for gentle cementing of rifts; too late for nicey-nice coddlings to do any good. Blame must be set and heads must roll. Onward then.

The first symptom of decay and dissolution is, of course, the rampant multitude of schizms and varieties of heretical sectarianism. A cult of pietist/gnostics has even sprung up whose object of devotion is "Bobra"! (Fine it may be to add emphasis to "Bob"'s female principle… but this is going too far. Here, however, is not the place to pick apart and scholasticize with all the latter-day tackers of thesi.) What we see is no less than the bastardization of the true doctrine, and this points to inexcusable laxity on the part of the Dallas Headquarters and even "Bob" himself. I warned against this years ago, but was ignored and reviled for my lack of faith. Perhaps a bit of history is in order.

I was of the original group of "Bob's" disciples. I wrote much of the now-destroyed early SubProp, and helped with all my might to build the underground apparatus into that mighty force it once was: the pride and envy of many a rival totalitarian group. But I warned against going aboveground with the Church, and I urged the Dallas chapter to jettison their plans for the Foundation. It was this that precipitated the brutal purge of myself and my followers, and although we remained close to "Bob" through secret correspondence, we were alarmed to note his increasing infatuation with the "Publickers," as we called them. Months before I died of a self-inflicted bullet wound to the head, I, with my comrades at The Word of Truth Ministries Reformed Church of the SubGenius (MiniTrue), had brought forth the Society of "Bob" in an attempt to wrest control away from the Publickers so that we might "go back below" for further learning and study before again attempting to actively proselytize. This project, the outreach to many splitfactions and SubTendrils, still holds much promise, and signs indicate that "Bob" is finally growing restive with the mediapink orientation of the Church.*

From the start I was anti-activist, and I called for the Church to shun involvement in projects before we were ready. The Word of "Bob" had to be installed with vigor among the ranks before we could undertake the vast efforts urged by "Bob." He had too much belief in us. I saw this, and so did he; for there is an over-eager "Bob" and an overcautious "Bob," an activist "Bob" and a passivist "Bob." Those who eagerly called for all-out, immediate war against the Pinks were obviously conspiracy infiltrators, and though we purged them in time, their close brethren were allowed to stay on and poison the air with whispered councils.

Even when the hierarchites call for peace and so on, when they tell us not to go overboard, they go too far. "Bob" save us from too-early recognition as a threat by the Conspiracy! We are not ready yet, not strong enough yet, to take Them on should They launch an offensive against us!

All to no avail. Catering to the whims of the dilute and the dissolute, Ivan Stang, Paul Mavrides and Philo Drummond all had "Bob's" ear, and he was swayed. There is a Quick Riches Scheme, they said, there is a Quick Victory Plan. We can find it only if we embark on the road now and cross the bridges when we come to them. In vain did I argue that we had maps of the territory, and that successful troops needed a battle plan, a strategic goal. "He wants us to sit on our behinds and talk until X-day," they told "Bob", souring him to my advice. Oh, evil lust! How can we achieve Slack when the opportunists offer up Slackless plan after Slackless plan? Work, work, and nothing but work have they produced for themselves, and for those confused few who thought they had the secrets.

And so. My prescription? How do we seal the yawning chasm between the Word and the practice? How do we oust the sectarian opportunists and at the same time unify the remaining dispersed forces? How do we rally?

From the start I want it known that my plan is only one among many, to be weighed for its merits and judged for its demerits. "Bob" will make a final pronouncement, and no matter what, we must follow him. But I believe he will see hope in what I offer.

I offer this: Since a few have, through their high placement within the Hierarchy, already obtained sensitive mailing lists and codes, we have already begun breaking ground for the Society of "Bob." This organ should work to overthrow the present opportunist leadership and establish an internal dictatorship of the SubGenius that will mirror, in embryo, the external goals that we pursue. Internal "Bob" world before external! That shall be our slogan in this fight. The dialogue forming the context within which this paper is presented should be the solid framework for a new rapprochement among the disaffected members of the SubGenius community. After a short period of debate during which everyone gets to air their views and proposals, and subsequent power struggle, a massive witch hunt should be conducted. All dissenters should be defined as enemies of "Bob" and then declared "open game" for the vicious subtlevenge organs of the Church. No matter what, our prime purpose is the exposure and vilification of "Bob" traitors.

The embryonic Society of "Bob" has already made successful outreach efforts and has established a working relationship with the violence prone clenches. The pacifist SubGenii have also been encouragingly approached, and both groups are convinced that this plan has merit. The Society was integral in organizing participation in this very project, including this publication of formerly suppressed dissenting opinion. A united "Bob" front! Slough off the Dallas Leaders for "Bob"!

We have sent a delegation to "Bob"'s mountain hideaway with a secret ultimatum, and should have gotten preliminary results around the time this document has been released.

Perhaps the Dallas Leaders for "Bob" will come around. If not, we shall see what we shall see. Adieu, then, for now.

Toward a Revitalized Church!
Internal "Bob" World Before External!
To Unity Behind "Bob"!

I have unavoidably given the barest skeleton brief of my whole case against the Church, and my prescription for a cure. This was planned. Nothing is more likely to attract serious consideration than a case made with all the cards laid out on the table, ace after ace—which illustrates, metaphysically, my case against the Church.

Prelude, True Anecdote and an Observation
for Kerry Wendell Thornley, fellow traveler.

My father told me once that going on the road meant waking up in some strange place twenty years later. Rub your eyes and wonder how you got stuck, where the time went. I was headed for Oregon then, Eugene to be exact, had briefed myself for the journey by rereading Kerouac.

He also told me that happiness is where you decide to find it, another platitude rendered obsolete through overuse, but it's something I forget too much anyway. During the blackouts I might less charitably say that I have been made to forget: a prelude to some low-key railing against circumstance or the laziness of my fellows. But I know about protesting too much; I see other people doing it all the time. When they won't stop I remind them that we see our worst in others.

This time I read Quixote to prepare myself; I've come that far. Staying in one place is anaesthetic. With it comes involvement, projects that pass the time to make up for any other prizes. The ones that glitter in proportion to their distance. I'd like to sleep for long periods of time, to have a check arrive every month, to rise only so I can make it to the Post Office before it closes and then answer my mail before going back to sleep. But I keep waking up, and the bed begins to gall me, there's no one there to call me back after I take a piss so I might as well stay up. I fall into ritual with ease and spend my free time in fierce argument with undisciplined old men, advocates of imposed order, taking the side of anarchy. I have been denounced in print, though.

Daisy didn't help much although she didn't suffer the standard setbacks. She had already made it to the next stage, where the problems are of a higher order. With a husband and child and a house to make payments on she didn't need me to provide commodities I couldn't afford. Others I hardly bother approaching. They leave too soon and follow the ones who never seem to make those biweekly poor decisions: lend ninety bucks here, pay the dental bill there, buy a hundred-lot of speeders to go. How do they manage to maintain those cars? And I know they can't. They're always broke on payday-plus-two the same as me.

But Daisy was demanding in an unsettling way. She challenged me with this tigress pose; just more codifications as far as I was concerned. Like some formular dance, step one, place foot here... This, and she vanished not long after the rebuff, family and all. Once, only once, my play came into it, and I told her I was busy the next time the doorbell rang. Right out of the blue, during timeout, she asked how big this Libertarian Party was for me.

"Well, I'm the newsletter editor… "

"You have the mailing list then."

"Just Wyoming." My bowels felt weak. My roommate never locked the back door even though I told him fifty times. "Mmm, kiss me," she purred. What power. She knows I know. That I won't, can't, do anything.

I think the honest cannot avoid making statements that earn them the greatest mistrust.

P.S. Daisy was una Cubana, her given name Josephine.

Untitled

It strikes me that facilitating the supercession of bourgeois social relations requires that we rally to the defense of the embattled system. Ardently. The more substantial our arguments in favor of people's indivisible right to live in abject intellectual poverty the quicker will our goal be accomplished, because while faint praise can damn, majestic eulogies can murder. Liberal humanist defenses of middle class virtue have succeeded largely because they are so trite, so banal, so ignorable. They put one to sleep; they do not fire the imagination either with intended horror or ostensible warm dedication. Thus the audience learns that there are defenders, which suffices; but not that the defenders are hiding behind a moral Maginot Line.

Sophisticated conservative defenses of just about anything are generally vulnerable because they tend to be condescending, patronizing, and compromising. They like Religion because it serves a useful purpose... and just like any utilitarian they'll succumb—or the line will succumb, while the conservatives will retreat and find new lies—when presented with an alternative.

Once we start judging Motherhood, Family, Breast-Feeding, and constitutional law on their relative merits, they are doomed. Relative merit is a function of Public Relations campaigns. They corrupt what they touch, which is good. One drawback is that they are gleefully inconsistent, which means we must be quick on our toes. They can defend Community better than any communist, or welfare with more sincerity than any liberal democrat who has dealt with the recipients—for whom he has developed a thinly veiled contempt.

STILL WONDE
TH

Weinberger blasts critics

Weinberger blasts Denmark

Carter blasts Reagan policies

Sheriff blasted

VIENNA, Austria (UPI) — Western psychiatrists blasted the "heinous" abuse of dissidents by the Soviet psychiatric profession Wednesday

Weinberger rips critic of military

Congressmen blast

Mondale blasts Rea

CHEYENNE — Gov. Herschler leveled a broadside Sen. Malcolm Wallop Thurs

Reagan commission

blasts anger Cody

Herschler blasts

G ABOUT
EW TERRAIN
OF THE
REVOLUTION?

"Every man must shout: there is great destructive, negative work to be done. To sweep, to clean. The cleanliness of the individual materializes after we're gone through folly, the aggressive, complete folly of a world left in the hands of bandits that have demolished and destroyed the centuries. With neither aim nor plan, without organization: uncontrollable folly, decomposition."
— Tristan Tzara

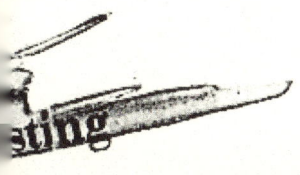

MINITRUE
P O Box 4081
Sheridan WY 82801

Doctor, Doctor, Fix Me Up

We left the stench of bodies, heat
of city afternoon, glare of glass, brute shape;
we left the clatter, horn, and screech…dull
ache in shoe, under hat. We left raw throat,
stale cigarette, cold pizza…
Or so we thought. We read the papers even
if we have no car, no telephone, no television.
All around us acquaintances tell of their *new* friend:
the desktop computer we just bought!
We only thought we had withdrawn; the cave turned into
prep room and we are left waiting, enervated,
sunk in age and sterile horror while the patient
ran off with the nurse. The prognosis was not good.
They'll be back but we'll be gone.

Untitled

the christian life: eagerly opting for banality

faith: consciously deciding in favor of ignorance

worship: freely chosen slavery

sacraments: sincere lying

tithes: reverse mugging, i.e. mugging yourself

religion: affirmative self-denial

church: empty halls where people pay to gather and celebrate their loneliness

confession: reporting one's obligatory disobedience

Punk, Meet Suburbanite

commodity, I'm just a commodity
so come on come on come on & use me

You didn't tell me you were going
didn't stop to say goodbye
we were getting pretty close, skip the bus, stay

I can tell you're starving
there's a concert tonight, plenty of tickets
let's negotiate. put together an economical package

I'll hang on your every word
grimace at the right moments
I'm interested in you. I'm your clown

I'll even dress up for you
mean but squeaky clean; my red brigades T shirt
we'll share a secret. The rest will stare

My X messed up my mind
it's tough living in the same town
Let's have a drink. Here, two hits of speed

I need a friend, a father-confessor
a foil to show me error
without the pain. for a moment together we can build
castles

I'm a good friend, yes
we'll have fun together, I can give you what you need

But your child. I know you need a man with money

I'll be a sport, we can relax
you won't be sorry
tell me, tell me. can I be your man?

I don't know yet, don't ask
I don't need sex to build those castles
Just talk. I'm alienated, draw me out

ask the right questions, make me see the humor
I just want to feel good for once
you can see, you're smart. can you bring me a new kind of love?

Cry. for me, so I can cry too. I feel your pain
but I can't do anything for it

I never cry

talk more then, it's what you want

I hate my job, my boss, my life
But I can't live your way
I can't give up. A little speed now & then, I'm 28 years old

the taxman is making me broke, they'll take my trailer house away
I have a kid to feed
I'm scared. Alone, and there's no help anywhere unless I sell myself

Chin up, my sweet, bravery will get us nowhere
god I know it's fucked
The Party is no answer. I won't push it on you

the future is dead you know
things will only get worse, let me cite statistics

I'm here. I wish I could fix it for you

Thanks for that, you know, there's no one else to tell this to
no one cares, they have their own troubles
I was seeing a shrink. But I followed your advice and quit

Let's laugh about it, please?
If we don't we'll kill ourselves
I'm a cynic on the outside. try harder, come up with an answer!

I think intimacy strengthens the walls
shuts out the externals
I'm not sure. But I think I lack it

You think I'd never marry you, probably right
who knows? but you've seen that dead end before
Never Again, you said. That's alright, though, it wouldn't help you

You're from another world, one I never knew
my mother was a strict baptist, tell me what you see from your vantage point

My turn to buy. Drink up there
I have no friends, only competitors and enemies
now you want sex
that will destroy my impartial companion. You understand don't you?

I understand. I've heard this before, every time in fact
I'm the hired escort, part of your jewelry
you need a gay man. did you think I was mr. right?

I don't intend to be mean, you can forgive my bitterness
you know what we're like

look. You know what signals you gave me

Yes, but I need someone to whom I can say: No
then I won't be cheap and easy: a slut without prospects
I don't want to drift downward, drink myself to death.
no, no, no!

The pain is so great I want to scream!
intimacy cannot help me, I have too much already
Don't make me a product! don't offer to buy me! I won't sell!

you're right. I counsel hate, rebellion, then.
you're right. I counsel nothing.
I'm slow, thickheaded. I wanted to be your commodity.

I want to die, to be resurrected, and to die again forever
I'm a machine. I'm dead already, you knew that
Buy me. Use me, throw me away

Nighttime for the Postman

The evening brings the toll of the bell,
From grassy knolls to communications hell —
Something's wrong, Captain!
Systems are down!
Lights are going *on* all over town!
Soon, too, like the breath of the night wind —
Sophocles heard it long ago —
Taxman, postman, draftboards glow…
One monopoly down — just a few more. You know,
Next week… *my* private link
I'll put my computer on line to think
Of ways to let my text go through
Out of the incompetent hands of you…

The Edwards Hotel
530 No. Main

"We don't want the insurance money."

"We're just ignorant white trash who had a streak of good luck, but don't worry — our family won't be rich for long." — Mr. & Mrs. Q.

DRUNKS & PSYCHOTICS WELCOME
You'll feel at home among your peers

Every Hour Is Happy Hour At
THE EDWARDS HOTEL!
530 N Main

RUN FOR OMNIPHOBIA

Sponsored by the Committee to Encourage Timorousness

Not much can be said for running...and that's not saying much. If anything, although joggers are contemptibly terrified of it, at least they <u>identify</u> the enemy, the abstract and concrete <u>totality</u>, by running away from it. They make the silence audible -- by plugging their ears. What about smashing the amplifiers? "They intoxicate themselves with work so they won't see how they really are."
-- Aldous Huxley.

In Method Acting, the student is taught that to feel the emotion, one should make the motion. It works both ways. Nothing is more obvious than that joggers are cultivating... fear. They lie to themselves about working at one's peak (after all, <u>who isn't</u> - and <u>who are they</u>?) thus disguising the desire to live forever that compensates them for the horror of an insipid present and the <u>real</u> activity it demands. We see the vain pursuit of physical "health" as overcompensation for mental debilitation, for paralyzed <u>will</u>. "One thing you can't hide...is when you're crippled inside..." --'Lennon. A land of cowards will always be able to sell itself accessories for the fashion conscious, cravenly fit. But will new tennis shoes cure their chronic cold feet?

Running is the acme of passivity, passivity so pure that for the runner, not even a static environment is banal enough to "permit" these inert morons to continue in servile receptivity. Your long-sought blankness even demands that you take a role...so you run, from nothing, to nothing. Joggers are whining, timid wimps.

You're never going to get the changes you need until you realize why you must stop running, and what it means...until you <u>real-ize</u> what it is you're incapable of facing up to: the necessity for all-encompassing revolution.

We're Gaining On You.

Letter from the Graveyard Shift

I've become jaded of late and convinced of the impossibility of achieving anything worthwhile. Concerning the modern state, I cannot see any way out or round or through, and it strikes me that one's time is better spent seeking after the little (and the great) pleasures of camaraderie, art and study.

Although not a mystic, I appreciate some of the tactical insights of Taoism...I think once the critique of organization is firmly assimilated, the whole political project of "anarchism" is exposed as a fraud. As anarchists: leafleting, speaking, proselytizing, agitating anarchists, we are continually trying to smooth over the inherent contradiction of trying to motivate people to act while disavowing any responsibility for their choice of action(s).

If we toss over organization and hierarchy (as we should) we are left without the prescriptive task of anarchist propaganda, and must face the emptiness of our individual lives, the emptiness that activity was intended to mask and failed to fill. There is still the joy of provoking and of communicating, but this begins more and more to fall into the older modes: humor and art.

We must stop thinking in terms of issues, power struggles, programs, policies, and projects (state and social) before we are going to be able to get anywhere, and this means an end to most of what the modern anarchist movement consists of.

Being an exemplary person is the most difficult thing; it is why so many of us are lured into prosperous schemes for publishing; promoting; and capitalizing on non-monetarily, of course, and discontent with a dying culture and an oppressed world. It vanishes into the mist on some rainy afternoon, and the aftertaste is bitter. But why, when grown, do we mourn for our childhood games? Let's invent new, better ones, that don't have this built-in self-destruct mechanism.

Publisher's Note

The following letter was Gerry Reith's final submission for *The Connection*, a long-running APA zine to which he was a frequent contributor. It appeared shortly after his death under the heading "The Usual" in issue #119 (dated April 29, 1984), where Reith's contributions were prefaced by Bob Black's memorial essay, "Occidental Death of an Anarchist."

As a segment in a thread of allied press correspondence, the text includes references to prior contributor questions and prompts that are beyond the scope of the present volume. While the broader context may be lost, the value of Reith's commentary on the then-impending publication of *Neutron Gun*, along with other relevant themes, seemed apposite to close the festivities.

The Usual

Neither/Nor says they are finally getting progress, and I read proof on about half the texts, so soon my book should be out and I'll be very happy if only because I'll feel vindicated for having so long pretended to write. I'll also be pleased at the inevitable bafflement in the ranks of the faintly hostile acquaintance local. I have a lot of confidence in this thing despite not believing it to be of any consequence greater than the consequence all tiny collections of shimmering literary jewels show a dearth of, and I suppose I should start planning how I'll celebrate arrival of copies. Go to the bar and wave it in people's faces? —naw, not unless you simultaneously cry words to the effect that you also wield a bottomless pocket... ON ME, FELLOWS! I'll get on the radio, that's what, and read excerpts and field stupid queries. Or maybe do nothing, except mention it to women in the bar: Yeah, I have a few copies at home if you'd like to come over...

This morning it is raining and on the way home the drops slid down the front of my shades, welling at the bottom. They're supposed to conceal, I thought. Why bother wearing them.

If it is training at all to play serious Chess daily for several months, which I have done, then the training will be in one's ability to maintain a sharp concentration. The rest of the phases are nothing now: the periods during which one spots Chess metaphors & apologies in everything... prosaic. For a long time I looked for a breakthrough, but it never came, and I slogged on, having early learned the lesson of humility and deciding that I wasn't in it to win any more, but to practice and enjoy it. 80% of the time when I face a worthy challenge, I lose miserably and for weeks prior to learning the lesson, I get on people's nerves. Exhaustion makes me irritable and enervation, nasty. Finally I developed the habit of smiling forcibly when I lost. In Method Acting: "To feel the emotion, make the motion." I am not a good player but I can honestly say I know good play when I see it. Memorizing the variations of a few openings taught principles of good opening play better than the formulaic advice of the classicists. I've improved, but the improvement hasn't come through any greater technical knowledge; it has come through a change in my emotional approach to the puzzles. A while back it became gossip that I am easy to beat but not when "he puts on his playing face." Now I wear it at But she's gone two weeks and the agony has persisted long enough to have become tolerable I suppose... Systems were down for a repair of circuits and the brownout is lifting, in some sectors. I cannot order my conclusions in any hierarchy of importance, but chief among the unpleasant experiences is that of establishing such a feedback loop as makes me feel like I've never once communicated with another person—and never will again—only to have the thing shut down... Like the lines are open but nothing is coming across the wires and my flywheels have been spinning in the red. No resolution, insufficient data, no conclusions, only tentatives, in chess: the myriad possible combinations...

In this respect I am struck by Diogenes'* use of a quote by da Vinci which strikes me as so alien and incomprehensible that its effect is only to inspire in me a revulsion for anyone who could think or say such a thing. I suppose it is reasonable to assume that this is the result calculated, and by past commentary on the matter by Dio we can assume that this is so; the apologetic and self-deprecating are, after all, begging to be rejected, a sign that they haven't been honest in presenting themselves as candidates for communion with another.

But the problem of promiscuity today is that "repressive" sexual mores serve another beneficial purpose beside the obvious ones related to health. In our existence we gain much by the consummation of community with others, and modern man whines endlessly about the alienation that is the lack of strong bonds between

---

* As context suggests, "Diogenes" here refers to the pen-name of fellow contributor to *The Connection*, not to the Greek Cynic. —Ed.

people. We're all painfully self-conscious Hamlets yearning after the kind of closeness only achieved in Conspiracy, love, or war. Political and criminal conspirators only persist once they've solved for themselves one of the age-old questions: that confronting recruiters when in need for a test for loyalty. Communion with another is proven by tests, and when sex no longer serves the extra purpose of sealing a pact—a multidimensional pact—then there is no longer any possible proof, and we are eternally separate despite all protestations to the contrary. Lesser proofs for lesser commitments do not suffice because we long for supreme unity; only a test built on a contrived resistance to an act will demonstrate, sacramentally, that here, and now, we have broken through and formed Conspiracy.

The trivialization of sex is a symptom of culture-wide infantilization in which we sell our birthright (no pun intended) for a delusory consolation prize. Furthermore, casual sex between friends no longer appeals to me, on the basis of my observation that while the friendship is colored by profundity betrayed, the Conspiracy is contradicted by cavalier attitude.

I've changed my mind on abortion, too, and now stand unequivocally opposed to it (although opposed yet to state intervention). The act not only bespeaks a loathsome trivialization, in constitutes perhaps one of the greatest possible indignities that a man can perpetrate on a member of the human species. And I'm not talking about the fetus, which I regard as an inconsequential adjunct to this aspect of the crime of abortion. That they will live if they are not aborted is merely good; (to digress, forever be damned the mouthings of psychotic liberals who bemoan abused children or the unwanted; they show that they understand Nothing of life, and confine us to the grim sight of a nation of chosen, coddled, and engineered little clones of Spock.) Returning, no imaginable horror short of torture-murder that could be conjured in Room 101—rats eating faces, whatever—could possibly match abortion for the degradation, the perversion, and the ugliness. And the anti-abortion cranks will win in the end, precisely on the basis of the aesthetic implications of the act. They are fighting on the front lines for the happy and useful pretension that Skinner and his ilk presume to be able to debunk with scornful science: that we are by nature dignified creatures and worthy. I would join the Church tomorrow if, in helping it succeed, I could know that the scientists would once again tremble in their laboratories and occasionally be brought to harsh task for their evil machinations. Unfortunately we live in a world demonic in its expectation that secular authority (or authority of any sort but the secular brand being particularly pernicious from this angle) deserves a fair—and long—test in the court of history. If only I could believe.

Phil, you asked me why I hate the world and would

relish its utter annihilation. The most I can say is that you've clearly got a long way to go before you learn where to edit yourself so as not to appear a fool. Your offers of riches, fame, and influence should I but quit complaining and go to work would entice the kind of retard who plays Supermarket Bingo. The only work worth working is to slay the dragon or follow Ulysses, and trapped as I am the best I can do is crawl through the mud of the psychosis called daily life and console myself with visions of mayhem, vengeance, riot, bombings, and instant death for those responsible for any specific crime. Bad Billy is a puerile liar and it hasn't taken him/her long to reveal it, but I think I've seen glimmerings that he/she at least would understand rage. Those who don't, I find, tend toward the smug & fatuous. In a less bitter mood I'll say I don't want to drive you away; I think you're okay really but I'm bugged by such a question. Forgive me. You're just a bit further down the road to realization of what a concentration-camp-world we live in. As a practicing phenomenologist, I know about the influence of mood over perception. The power of negative thinking has proven itself far more effective than that of your positive kind in the past, if only because positive thinking is a subset of critical intelligence in general, a special case that posits dangerous editing of input.

Joe Fulks: Your mention of multi-model communication to TC118 was fortuitous considering that this same issue contained my minimalist-metafiction masterpiece, "Twilight to Authority." I hope Kysor scratches his head although I expect him to be a clod about it, as most of your semi-educated techies tend to be. What they don't realize is that metafiction truly serves up more precision than fiction itself, and is often criticized by the "humanists" of the art community for being sterile, overly-technical to the point of being nothing beyond dazzling technique, etc., etc. Pynchon, the greatest writer of all time, wrote technical manuals for Boeing while he was at work on *V.*, and trained in mathematics if I remember aright.

GERRY REITH BIBLIOGRAPHY
Compiled by Bob Black

"Anarchfesto Critique" (letter). *Anarchy: A Journal of Desire Armed* n6 (Aug 1985): p. 6.

"Bad Company" (review of Niven and Pournelle, *Oath of Fealty*). *Prometheus* v.2, n2 (April 1984): pp. 4–5.

"Being Against Motherhood Does Not Go Over in Peoria." *Inside Joke* n13 (July 1983): p. 19.

"Case Studies." *A Good Day to Die*, ed John Bennett. Ellensburg Washington: Vagabond Press, 1985: pp. 55–58.

"Case Studies." *Inside Joke* n3 (Aug 1982): pagination unknown.

"Closing Redux." *Inside Joke* n24 (Sept 1983): p. 4.

"Communication." *Inside Joke* n8 (March 1982): pagination unknown.

"Conflicting Virtues." *Inside Joke* n8 (March 1982): pagination unknown.

"Cost/Benefit Equations." *The Death Collection* ed. Gregory Altreuer. Ann Arbor: Neither/Nor Press, April 1982, pp. 8, 10, 12, 14.

"The Devil's Day Off." *Inside Joke* n11 (June 1982): pp. 9–10.

"The Devil's Day Off." *The Moorish Science Monitor* v11, n8 (Winter 1987/1988): unpaginated.

"Digressions." *The Connection* n119 (April 29, 1984): pp. 21–22

"Doctor, Doctor, Fix Me Up" (poem). *Seditious Delicious* n1 (Winter 1984): unpaginated.

"Drifting in One Spot I." *Inside Joke* n26 (Nov 1983): p. 8.

"Drifting in One Spot II." *The Connection* n119 (April 29, 1984): pp. 18–20.

"Drifting in One Spot II." *Minifictions Five* (1984): pagination unkknown.

"The Edwards Hotel." *The Connection* n115 (Nov 6, 1983): p. 73.

"The Epistle of Gerry to the Connectors, Section Seven." *The Connection* n115 (Nov 6, 1983): pp. 61–62.

"Errata." *The Connection* n116 (Dec 18, 1983): pp. 59–60.

"Explaining 'Bob'—And Other Matters of Critical Importance." *The Connection* n107 (Oct 23, 1982): pp. 58–60.

"Foreign Policy." *Anarchy: A Journal of Desire Armed* n9 (Dec 1985/Jan 1986): pp. 4–5.

"Formulas." *The Connection* n119 (April 29, 1984): pp. 23–24.

"Fraud, Cheat, Lie, Thrill." *Inside Joke* n16 (Dec 1982): pagination unknown.

"Future Thoughts 1." *Inside Joke* n19 (March 1983): pagination unknown.

"Gerry Reith on *Processed World*." *Frefenzine* n58 (April 19, 1986): unpaginated.

"Gerry Reith on *Procesed World*." *SRAFBull* n94 (April/May 1986): p. 12.

"Ignore the Five." *The Spark* v1 n2 (Sept-Oct 1983): unpaginated.

"Issues in Suspension." *The Connection* n135 (April 27, 1986): p. 78.

"Issues in Suspension." *Mallife* n11 (Winter 1986): unpaginated.

"Issues in Suspension." *Nightmares of Reason* n3 (1987): unpaginated.

"An Introduction to SubGenius Theology: Brief Examination

of Several Doctrinal Points." *The Stark Fist of Removal* v17, n39 (1982): pp. 21-22.

"K. goes to the Lecture." *Inside Joke* n7 (Jan 1983): pagination unknown.

"Kidnapped!" *The Stark Fist of Removal.* v17, n41 (1984): p. 35.

Letter to Freddie Baer quoted (slightly abridged) in Bob Black "Occidental Death of an Anarchist." *The Connection* n119 (April 20, 1984): pp. 9-12.

Letter. *Rhubarb.* v1, n4 (March 5, 1983): p. 7.

Letter to "Mom, Dad, Sis, Bro." *SRAFBull* n81 (not dated): unpaginated.

Letter to "Opposers." *SRAFBull* n76 (Sept 1982): unpaginated.

Letter "To the Roundtable." *SRAFBull* n78 (Dec 1982): unpaginated.

Letter "To whom it may concern." *SRAFBull* n85 (not dated): unpaginated.

Letter. *The Stark Fist of Removal.* v17, n41 (1984): 92.

"Letter From the Graveyard Shift." *OVO* n1 (1986): unpaginated.

"Letter From the Graveyard Shift." *SRAFBull* n96 (Aug-Sept 1986): pp. 2, 15.

"Letter from the Graveyard Shift." *Vultur* n1 (Spring 1985): p. 3. (French translation, "Lettre d'outre tombe," at p. 11).

"Libertarian for Hire." *The Connection* n119 (April 29, 1984): pp. 16-17.

"Manifesto Notes, 1." *Inside Joke,* n22 (June 1983): p. 11.

"The Mechanics of TC — a note." *The Connection* n110 (March 6, 1983): pp. 53-56, 61.

"Melpomne's Little Sister Georgene." *Inside Joke* n29

(Winter-Spring 1984): pagination unknown.

"My Contribution for the Next Issue. . ." *The Connection* n111 (April 16, 1983): pp. 67–71.

Neutron Gun: Assembled by Gerry Reith. Ann Arbor/New York: Neither/Nor Press. 1985. (Reith Texts: "Warning, You Have Just Entered an Advanced Sector"; "To Rust Unburnished"; "Kings of Orient, Dresden, D.C."; "Fraud, Cheat, Lie, Thrill"; "Foreign Policy"; "John's Adventure"; "Cost/Benefit Equations"; and "Twilight to Authority."

Neutron Gun: Assembled by Gerry Reith. Second Edition. Ann Arbor/New York: Neither/Nor Press. (Reith Texts, in addition to those in the First Edition: "Run for Omniphobia"; second frontispiece; "Truth is Lies"; end page; "Gerry Reith's Post-Mortem Addendum"; and an untitled cartoon.

"Nighttime for the Postman" (poem). *Seditious Delicious* n4 (Autumn 1984): unpaginated.

"Not[e] on the Impossibility of Reading Your Way to Liberty." *The Spark* v1, n5 (May-June 1984): unpaginated.

"Number 8, Number 8." *Inside Joke* n19 (March 1983): p. 8.

"An Objective Lesson." *Inside Joke* n22 (July 1983): p. 25.

"On *Processed World*." *The Connection* n133 (Jan 27, 1986): p. 118.

"Opombe k tezi, da je v svobodo nemogoce priti z branjem" (pp. 86–89); "Kritica anarchista" (pp. 100–101); "Johnova dogodivscina" (pp. 107–120); "Polemika proti novopisu" (pp. 129–130), in *Pozdravi iz Babilona* ed Bob Black and Gregor Tomc. Ljubljana, Yugoslavia: Knjiznica Revolucionae Teorije, 1987. (Slovene translations of "Note on the

Impossibility of Reading Your Way to Liberty," "An anarchfesto Critique," "John's Adventure," and "Polemic Against NeWrItE," respectively.)

"The Opposite of the Exit." *The Connection* n112 (May 30, 1983): pp. 40-44. (With two letters to newspapers at p. 44.)

"The Pleasure Palace, A Visit." *Inside Joke* n9 (April 1983): p. 7.

"Prelude, True Anecdote, and an Observation." *Inside Joke* n10 (May 1982): p. 8.

"Quixote: How to Use." *A Good Day to Die*, ed John Bennett. Ellensburg Washington: Vagabond Press, 1985: pp. 60-62.

"Quixote: How to Use." *BVI Pacifica* v2, n2 (1986-1987): pp. 25-27.

"Quixote: How to Use." *Digressive Dialogues* n1 (June 1, 1987): pp. 6-7.

"Revisionist History for Children." *Inside Joke* n25 (Oct 1983): pagination unknown.

"Rodeo Week in Sheridan," *The Connection* n135 (April 27, 1986): p. 77.

"Rodeo Week in Sheridan." *Mallife* n11 (Winter 1986): unpaginated.

"Rodeo Week in Sheridan." *Philly Zine* (1987): unpaginated.

"The Roots of Modern Terror." *Between the Lines* n5 (date unknown): p. 4.

"The Roots of Modern Terror." *The Stark Fist of Removal* v17, n40 (1983): p. 29.

"The Roots of Modern Terror." *X It Out* n3 (Sept-Oct 1986): p. 24.

"Run for Omniphobia." *The Connection* n114 (Sept 1983): p. 71.

"Run for Omniphobia." in *Semiotext[e] USA* ed Jim Fleming and Peter Lamborn Wilson. New York: Autonomedia, Inc., 1987: p. 296.

"Science Fiction: Qverrated." *Frefenzine* n58 (April 19, 1986): unpaginated.

"Singularity." *The Connection* n135 (April 27, 1986): pp. 77-78.

"Singularity." *Mallife* n11 (Winter 1986): unpaginated.

"Singularity." *Nightmares of Reason* n3 (1987): unpaginated.

"Start at the Beginningngnow." *The Connection* n114 (Sept 11, 1983): pp. 69-70.

"That Then I Scorn to Change My State." *Inside Joke* n14 (Sept 1982): pagination unknown.

"There Is No Autonomy Without Authority." *SRAFBull* n83 (not dated): unpaginated.

"These Ideas Are in Everyone's Heads." *The Connection* n106 (Sept 12, 1982): 45-47.

"Three Men in Dresden." *Inside Joke* n7 (Feb 1982): p. 11.

"Twilight to Authority." *The Connection* n118 (March 1984): pp. 95-97.

Untitled parable beginning "Diligent Historians..." *Not Mellow* (not dated): unpaginated.

Untitled Staffer Autobiography. *Inside Joke* n17 (Jan 1983): p. 3.

"USA Sucks/USSR No. 1!" (poster). *False Positive* n2 (late 1984): p. 19.

"The Usual." *The Connection* n119 (April 29, 1984): pp. 13-15.

"Variations on a Theme." *Inside Joke* n21 (May 1983): p. 9.

"What's the News, Blues?" *The Connection* n113 (July 23, 1983): pp. 70-73.

"Winning Hearts and Minds." *Anarchy: A Journal of Desire Armed* n11 (April 1986): p. 9.

"Winning Hearts and Minds." *Philly Zine* n5 (1988): unpaginated.

"Winning Hearts and Minds." *A Good Day to Die*, ed John Bennett. Ellensburg Washington: Vagabond Press, 1985. pp. 52-54.

Caveat Lector.

www.NineBandedBooks.com